LEARNING
STRATEGIES
for MUSICAL
SUCCESS

BY MICHAEL GRIFFIN

Published by Music Education World
Adelaide, Australia
www.musiceducationworld.com
First Published 2013
Copyright © 2013 Michael Griffin
All rights reserved.

ISBN: 1481946730
ISBN-13: 9781481946735

For my mother and uncle, Josephine Griffin and Trevor Gibbons, who inspired me to persist with, and gain enjoyment from, the study and performance of music.

V

CONTENTS

FIGURES

FOREWORD

Every serious music student, music teacher, and parent of a music student will find important information in this book about what it takes to succeed as a performer. Michael Griffin brings together a broad range of information from science, sport, the lives of notable performers, and his own experience teaching in many different schools and countries and performing professionally around the world. His workshops and lectures on teaching and learning music are highly acclaimed.

In discussing musical potential, Griffin presents a very interesting perspective on the learning processes of Beethoven, Mozart, John Coltrane, Charlie Parker, The Beatles, and other musicians. He also discusses ideas from Albert Einstein, Carol Dweck, and Muhammad Ali. I can't think of any other book that draws on all of these resources to create a new understanding of learning music.

The concept of talent and intelligence is widely misunderstood. Griffin debunks the theory that you either have talent or you don't and that intelligence is fixed and can be measured by one test. Believing this leads to the tragic idea that there's no point in working hard. This is very important information for parents, students, and teachers.

Of course practice is important, but there are many different ways to practise. In this book Griffin explains these methods. When one plans to spend thousands of hours doing something, it surely is worth knowing how to use the time most effectively.

Although the focus here is on music, the information and ideas also apply to learning in other areas. The scientific research that this is based on is interpreted in a way that is easily understood. Griffin gives clear examples of how concepts are applied that make for enjoyable reading.

This book has a potential for making lifelong differences in the lives of music students, parents and teachers.

Roy E. Ernst, PhD, LLD
Professor Emeritus,
Eastman School of Music of The University of Rochester
Founder, New Horizons Music

INTRODUCTION

Learning Strategies for Musical Success presents an overview of concepts that will enhance the lifelong enjoyment of learning music and is geared toward classroom and studio music teachers, music students, and parents. Samuel Johnson once said, "People need to be reminded more often than they need to be instructed," and these pages serve this purpose. But good teaching is not always intuitive and is sometimes carried out with the best of intentions at the expense of learning. Periodically teachers and learners need reinvigoration and inspiration. In this book I share exciting new findings in learning psychology and cognitive neuroscience that will inform and improve the learning of music. Just as the music student embarks on a lifelong journey for musical understanding, the music teacher is challenged to embrace an enduring search for teaching methods that result in more successful learning outcomes.

Chapter One

Musical Potential

"Prince, what you are you are by accident of birth; what I am, I am through my own efforts. There have been thousands of princes and will be thousands more, but there is only one Beethoven!" [1]

Ludwig van Beethoven showed scant respect for those who generated their sense of worth through birthright alone. In his eyes, effort and perseverance were the keys to mastery, but not everyone believes this. Some people subscribe to the theory that superior achievement is part of a genetic endowment. Most people believe it is a mixture of nature and nurture. Logically, knowledge and ability can only derive from genetic endowment or living experience. One problem with gene theory is that researchers have yet to find talent genes among the twenty thousand or so genes with which we are evidently born. If musical talent or any other talent is innate then there must be a gene for it. Talent genes may well be discovered in the future but if not and thus do not exist, then where does musicality emanate? Can something come from nothing? Is talent a gift from God? Homer seemed to think so. [2] To this day musical ability is more often considered innately derived than any other ability or human faculty (1). According to talent theory, some lucky individuals win the genetic lottery. They are born with musical

---

1   Beethoven: The Man and the Artist, as Revealed in his Own Words.
2   In the *Odyssey*, Homer writes, "Call in the inspired bard, Demodocus. God has given this man the gift of song."

talent and fortunate circumstances allow them to find opportunities to nurture this gift early in their lives. Evidence for this is anecdotal and stories of exceptional prodigies abound. How, for example, could Mozart's precocity be explained in any other way?

Actually, Mozart's musical feats can be explained rationally. It is difficult to separate fact from fiction 230 years after the event, but several factors do help account for his accomplishments. Mozart was immersed in a concentrated musical environment from his earliest days. His father, Leopold, was an excellent music educator and took every opportunity to earnestly promote his son's musical ability. Stories such as that of two-year-old Wolfgang identifying the sound of pig squeals as G-sharp should be taken with a grain of salt, as they were most likely spawned by his father, who was not always honest in relation to his son where music was concerned. Leopold was known to subtract a year from the ages of his children, Wolfgang and Nannerl, when advertising their performances (2). Leopold was a smart operator. He knew that lowering his children's ages would augment their appeal and perhaps enhance his own reputation as a teacher; it is not unusual for parents to embellish facts to help their children get ahead. A closer inspection of Mozart's childhood compositions indicates assistance from his father as well as thematic material borrowed from other composers, notably Johann Christian Bach, with whom Mozart collaborated in London at the age of nine. If we accept that these are normal processes that lead to achievement, even extraordinary achievement, then none of this is an issue. Imitation is a natural part of the learning process, and lying about a child's age does not detract from the skills exhibited. However, it does skew the picture. The possibility that Mozart's great desire to make music was rooted in pre-birth fortune cannot be ruled out, but his early musical environment was encouraging and inspiring. Having a great passion for music—and an overbearing, micro-managing father—led him to practise for several hours a day from the age of three. [3] Mozart took advantage of the many opportunities afforded him.

---

3   In *Genius Explained,* Michael Howe estimates that Mozart accrued about 3,500 hours of practice by age six.

Even if you take the position that a child is born with genetic potential, this potential can only become skill and ability through work. As John Maxwell implies in the title of his book *Talent Is Never Enough*, major achievement requires preparation and persistence on top of any natural potential. This is most true as we progress in our skills. The assumed natural talent that differentiates children becomes less evident as they age, as dedication and sheer hard work play greater roles in achievement. Malcolm Gladwell says, "The further a career develops, the less important the role of assumed innate ability in comparison with preparation or practice" (3). Quality and quantity of practice develop expertise.

In the investigation of superior achievement, precocity can be explained in terms of practice hours, opportunity, parental support, and a young starting age. What distinguishes prodigies is the fact that they are constantly compared with children their own age, rather than with others who have accrued similar quantities of practice hours, similar opportunities, and family support. Take Tiffany Poon for example. Born in Hong Kong in 1997, this girl has experienced a meteoric rise as a concert pianist and has been lauded far and wide for her giftedness and substantial accomplishments. No doubt it is rare to find a child her age who has achieved so much and who plays the piano so well. At the age of eight, Tiffany accepted the opportunity of a scholarship at The Juilliard School in New York City, and flourished. As is usually the case with young achievers, testimonials on her website make age comparisons.

> Tiffany Poon possessed skills of a kind that I had never observed in such a young musician. She displays a sense of musical maturity that goes well beyond her current age.
> -Gary McPherson, Ormond Chair of Music, Head of the School of Music, University of Melbourne

> Tiffany Poon plays with technical skills well beyond her years.
> -the *Columbus Dispatch*

Tiffany's biography states that she started playing on a toy piano at the age of two and when she began formal lessons at age four-and-a-half she practised four hours a day for the next two years. If we assume

Tiffany had a rest day and practised six days per week, this totals 1,248 hours of practice. This is substantial for one so young and is many times the practice hours of other children of that age. Assuming that fifteen minutes is about the average daily practice time for this age group, we have a 1,600 percent differential in practice time. Professor John Sloboda says, "There is no evidence of a fast track for high achievers," which suggests that in terms of time expenditure, the pathway to progress is basically the same for everyone. To achieve you must put in the hours and do the work. In one study Sloboda found that predominantly it takes individuals about 1,200 practice hours to reach a formal music examination level of Grade Five (4). Accumulation of practice hours is not the only factor in musical achievement, but it is the predominant one.

We owe it to Tiffany to give *her* the credit for having achieved excellence. As an infant she had an intense curiosity for music and quickly developed the ability to concentrate for long periods of time. Note also that the testimonial from the *Columbus Dispatch* refers to 'technical' skills. Fields such as music, chess, and mathematics are suited to young achievement because the precocity is almost always derived from algorithmic study. In later life real musicianship requires much more than technical prowess. Adult musicians with technical skills alone are not special. Tiffany's parental support also has significantly influenced her achievement. Not only did the family relocate from Hong Kong for the express purpose of gaining a better music education for Tiffany, but Tiffany's parents also instilled in her the critical learning strategies we call *deliberate practice*. From the earliest stages of Tiffany's musical development her mother challenged her to play through passages several times correctly in succession. This game taught Tiffany the power of repetition. Contrast this with how most children practise music. One study found that more than 90 percent of children's practice time was spent playing pieces from beginning to end only once and without stopping to correct any errors (5). In their coaching, Tiffany's parents showed great astuteness, especially considering neither of them had any formal musical training.

Carol Dweck predicts developmental problems for students praised for innate talent rather than effort. Dweck's research, as documented in her book *Mindset: The New Psychology of Success* presents a strong case that a focus on genetic gift can lead to a poor work ethic. Children with this *fixed-intelligence mindset* get the impression that they do not need to work as hard as 'average' children do. This leads to a tendency to give up easily when obstacles arise, because with this mindset, difficulties signify a lack of true ability and come as a shock to the ego. After all, if you are gifted at something, things should come naturally and you should not have to work too hard for them. People labelled as 'naturally talented' or 'gifted' can be ruthlessly protective of their labels and therefore avoid challenges or risks that might lead to their making mistakes. Their labels must be preserved at all costs. On the other hand, people who believe their intelligence is a potential to be developed through effort are less worried about short-term mistakes, difficulties, and failures. They view these events as an essential part of the learning process. People with this *growth-intelligence mindset* tend to reach higher levels of achievement and enjoy the learning challenges inherent in the process.

Research into the effects of mindset on achievement is of particular interest to music educators. Susan O'Neill found noticeable differences in the practice efficiency among children exhibiting different mindsets (6). [4] For one, fixed-intelligence-mindset children practised roughly twice as much as growth-intelligence-mindset children to reach the same level of moderate performance achievement. Evidently fixed-intelligence-mindset children use their time less efficiently. Given what we know about fixed-intelligence-mindset behaviour, it is plausible that these children might avoid practising pieces or passages that pose particular difficulties. These children probably spend more time on what they already can play well, which might be enjoyable but will hardly improve performance. Growth-intelligence-mindset children are more likely to embrace the challenges that lead to mastery. It is not easy to teach learning strategies to fixed-intelligence-mindset students who have deep-set beliefs about their potential. By attributing failure to lack of effort or poor practice,

4   Another Susie O'Neill, an Australian Olympic swimming champion, referred to these mindset issues when analysing Australia's poor performance at the 2012 London Olympics.

however, teachers and parents can change this mindset. Stressing the importance of effort rather than natural ability is paramount.

Confidence is central in positive psychology. It centres on self-belief in one's ability to achieve certain goals. If confidence results from progress through effort, it has enormous worth. The level of confidence prior to a performance examination can help predict a subsequent examination result. When taking examinations, students with a high level of confidence outperform their peers with similar skills but lower expectations (7). These students are confident that their work ethic will yield positive results so they persist with training in the face of obstacles. Confidence is clearly important; as Robert Sternberg says, "The best predictor of success among students is in their belief in their ability to succeed" (8). Top-performing athletes spend a great deal of time cultivating an indomitable spirit of self-belief. Perhaps no other sportsperson exemplified this to the degree of heavyweight boxer and Athlete of the Century Muhammad Ali. [5] Prior to a bout, Ali stood before the media shouting, "I am the greatest." Some viewed his actions as egotistical, even comical, but the power that accompanied Ali's confidence was extraordinary. Action follows feeling. [6] Muhammad Ali's self-belief was essential for his performance, and he used repetition to cultivate it to an extraordinary level.

> *It is the repetition of affirmations that leads to belief. Once that belief becomes a deep conviction, things begin to happen.*
> *- Muhammad Ali*

When Ali was in Australia for the 2000 Sydney Olympics, I performed at a cocktail party in his honour and was able to meet and talk with him. What a commanding and inspiring presence he was. We talked about music and charity. Ali's favourite music was that of The Beatles, and he believed that doing good works was his religious obligation.

---

5   *Sports Illustrated* magazine awarded Ali this title in 1999.

6   This is a principle put forward by Harvard psychologist William James. James said it also works the other way—if you deliberately act, feelings will follow. Action and feelings go together.

A focus on fixed-talent is common in the world of sport, and with some justification, because unlike the music gene, physical genes are known to exist. In the 2010 Football World Cup, titleholder Italy was supremely confident of their ability to defeat semi-professional New Zealand, so much so that pre-match media comments revealed arrogance and contempt for the skill level of their opponent. Given that on the world market one Italian player was worth three times the value of the New Zealand team, Italy's attitude was explainable. However, Italy failed to defeat New Zealand and soon after was out of the World Cup. Italy's problem was a focus on natural ability. The New Zealand team focussed on work ethic. Passion, the first step in achievement, can outperform talent.

A fixed-intelligence mindset stifles progress and leads to underachievement, lower practice motivation, and ineffective practice strategies. A change of mindset opens the door of possibility; the musicians who end up being brilliant and expert are those who work the hardest and the smartest. This is the level playing field.

There are many ways to be musical. Sight-reading ability, playing by ear, memorising music, improvising, creating, expressing, and dexterous displays of virtuosity are some of the diverse manifestations of musicality. Few people develop the multifaceted strengths of overall musicianship because of the time investment required to develop each strand. Even some great composers, despite the fertility of their musical minds, were not necessarily expert in a technical or performance sense. The general community definition of musicality is narrow. Those the public consider musical play an instrument, sing to a good standard, or compose. Being musical, however, is also about the response of the listener. Rather than endorsing a model of musical exclusivity, a broader definition embraces the wider community and encourages greater musical exploration.

The refrain 'I'm not musical' cheapens human capacity. We are all musical, as is obvious by the inordinate amounts of time people devote listening to music. American adolescents, for example, listen to more than seven hours of music each day (9). Being musical is the normal human condition but dazzling displays of technical virtuosity distort our understanding of musicality. Daniel Levitin says, "The chasm between musical experts and everyday musicians has grown so wide in our culture that people feel discouraged" (10). This, he says, "has grown out of the nineteenth-century tradition of the European virtuoso, where the technical aspects of performance were valued above all else, and performance was considered a specialist skill." Assuming that the normal cognitive and physical functions are in order, everyone can learn to play music. Rather than being a gift bestowed upon a chosen few, the ability to make music is a special feature of our humanity and is within us all. Our greatest gift is our capacity to learn. "We are born to learn," said Aristotle, and this includes learning music. Quantities of quality practice can transform a person of seemingly average aptitude into a much improved and possibly outstanding performer. Generations of future music learners face the educational consequences of adult mindsets, so we must debunk talent myths and embrace growth through effort.

High Expectations

Children often aim high and like to distinguish themselves through excellence. The benefits of excellence are numerous. Indeed many of life's experiences, opportunities, and jobs are only available to individuals who have achieved a high level of expertise. We feel proudest of the achievements for which we have worked hardest, and reflecting on past success gives us a perpetual sense of satisfaction and hope. New success allows us to view our self-image in a fresh and more favourable light, and new possibilities emerge as excellence begets excellence. Ron Berger states, "Excellence is transformational. Once the student sees what s/he is capable of, that student is never quite the same. There is a new self-image, a new notion of possibility, a new appetite for excellence (11)".

How does one become an expert in music? We know experts work and practise much harder than the average skilled person, but the assumption of an equal or greater genetic contribution still prevails in common thought. The relationship between general intelligence as measured by IQ tests and exceptional performance in any specific domain has been found to be rather weak. However, a much stronger predictor for expertise has been discovered. Cross-domain-expertise researchers have come up with a minimum number of hours required for one to attain 'expert' status.

Ten Thousand Hours

> *"Genius! For thirty-seven years I have practised fourteen hours a day, and now they call me a genius." - Pablo de Sarasate*

How long does it take to become an expert? Daniel Levitin says, "The emerging picture is that ten thousand hours of practice is required to achieve the level of mastery associated with being a world-class expert" (10). Ten thousand hours of practice amounts to two hours and forty-five minutes of practice per day, every day, for ten years. Daniel Coyle says, "The true expertise of a genius is in their ability to practise obsessively" (12). Geoffrey Colvin endorses this theme. "The conventional wisdom on natural talent is a myth; the real path to great performance is a matter of choice" (1). Listen to experts in our society. They explain their achievement in terms of their sense of curiosity as well as their struggle, determination, perseverance, doggedness, self-discipline, and hard work.

> *Thou, O God, who sellest us all good things at the price of labour.*
> *- Leonardo da Vinci*

Experts who have invested fewer than ten thousand hours are proving difficult to find, and in some disciplines, notably the virtuosic stage of the concert pianist and violinist, the hours required for international expertise are significantly more than ten thousand. The unique physical requirements of these instruments seem to demand more practice hours than most other instruments (13).

In his book *Outliers*, Malcolm Gladwell cites examples of successful people who accumulated ten thousand hours in their formative years.

His stories serve to encourage students to work hard to realise their aspirations. We want children to believe in their ability to improve through regular training for a sustained period of time. Thomas Carlyle said, "Genius is the infinite capacity to take pains." [7] The pathway to expertise, however, requires too much commitment for most people. If it were easy, there would be many more experts. For those who are prepared to endure the discomfort referred to by Carlyle, distinction is possible. I read biographies of great achievers- musicians in particular. What most interests me is their practice habits, level of family and community support, and early opportunities. Let us examine the work ethic of some renowned experts.

When Paul Desmond interviewed alto saxophonist Charlie Parker in 1954, he asked him how he acquired his 'fantastic technique." Parker responded, "I cannot see that there's anything fantastic about my progress at all, Paul. I put quite a bit of study into the horn, that's true. So much so that on one occasion the neighbours asked my mother to move. They said I was driving them crazy with the horn. I used to put in at least eleven to fifteen hours every day, and I did this over three to four years."[8]

Take the midpoints of Parker's practice account. If he practised six days a week with four weeks off per annum for rest and rehabilitation, we can calculate the following.

13 hours per day x 6 (days per week) x 48 (weeks per year) x 3.5 years = 13,104 hours

According to this estimate, Charlie Parker accrued well over ten thousand hours in three-and-a-half years. His practice routine was consistent and sustained so from his perspective progress was measured and incremental.

Another jazz saxophonist, John Coltrane, took up the alto horn in 1939 and become known as one of—if not the most—prolific 'practisers'

7   *History of Frederick II of Prussia, Called Frederick the Great*, written 1858–65.
8   This is recorded online http://www.puredesmond.ca/pdbird.htm

ever. Coltrane had an insatiable appetite for musical development, and some stories have him practising up to sixteen hours a day. Very few musicians practise between sets during a performance, but Coltrane did. People said that if you drove past Coltrane's house, "If the lights are on, he's practising. If not, he's asleep or on the road." Coltrane's technique was one of the finest examples of polished dexterity in any discipline. He did not start out a 'natural' but he worked at it.

Lewis Porter says the following about Coltrane:

He was, rather, someone who did not begin with obvious exceptional talent, and that makes his case all the more interesting. One can become one of the great musicians of all time and not start off as some kind of prodigy. The process of development and education is the same for people of spectacular achievement—geniuses if you will—as for everyone else. They too exchange ideas with friends and colleagues. Coltrane was not some isolated genius but a normal person growing and developing in a fortunately inspired circle of musicians (14).

Robert Weisberg's analysis of The Beatles details the astonishing hours they spent prior to hitting the big time.

Beginning in mid-1960, when they were known only around Liverpool, they were performing approximately four hundred times per year on average; that is, more than once per day. Based on records of the performances, one can estimate that the total amount of time they spent onstage during those years, without taking into account any offstage rehearsal and practice at all, approached two thousand hours. Thus, when they burst on the scene, they were already seasoned professionals, and that seasoning had come about through practice (15).

The Beatles spent their early years playing the musical works of others. Most of their repertoire was Top 40 cover songs, and they played these repeatedly. When The Beatles started to write their own songs, they borrowed their ideas from other artists. Their early song-writing attempts were not hits, and most have been forgotten.

Ludwig van Beethoven practised many hours a day at the age of four. As a youth he once told his teacher, the renowned composer Carl Czerny, "I practise stupendously, often till past midnight." Beethoven continually questioned the status quo in his search for musical meaning and new ideas. His persistent curiosity, together with a strong presence of mind, shaped his desire to explore. Beethoven secretly sought out alternative tutoring at the same time he was having lessons with the conservative Joseph Haydn.

Beethoven recorded his musical ideas in manuscript sketchbooks. The fact that he was a harsh self-critic is evident in the pages of the fifty of these books found following his death. In many cases the initial themes were of mediocre quality but were altered and reworked again and again in a process of continuous improvement. Beethoven was not a quick worker, and he laboured with the initial creation, design, and craftsmanship of his ideas. Like most men and women of genius, he worked with a ferocity and intensity. Beethoven was a man of perseverance, industry, and endeavour. These were the catalysts for his achievement.

In 1987 psychologist K. Anders Ericsson went to Berlin for two years to conduct research into the achievement of violinists. His aim was to investigate correlation between the standard of graduation performance and the numbers of hours practised. Ericsson divided the violinists' proficiency into the following categories: world-class, very good, competent, and amateur. He then calculated the students' total lifetime practice hours. The violinists in the study all had begun tuition at about the age of five and practised roughly the same amount in the first few years. From about the age of eight, their practice habits changed dramatically. The results of the study were astonishing. Ericsson found that by the age of twenty, the violinists who were classified as world-class had practised for at least ten thousand hours. Violinists considered excellent had practised roughly eight thousand hours. Competent violinists perhaps at the level of a teacher had practised about five thousand hours, and good amateurs approximately two thousand hours. The relationship between expertise and hours practised was predictive and the 'ten thousand hour-rule' was born (16).

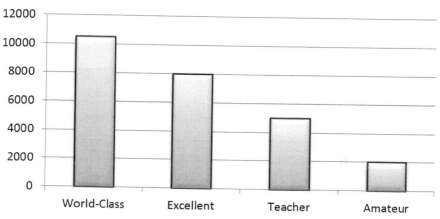

Ericsson's Study on Berlin Violinists

Figure 1: Expertise and Hours Practised, Ericsson

This seminal study found a statistically significant correlation between practice time and performance standard. Ericsson also found that the best musicians engaged in a certain type of focussed practice, which he called *deliberate practice*. Resembling Carlyle's 'pain' of genius Ericsson posits that deliberate practice requires a type of effort that is not necessarily enjoyable. What people do enjoy, however, is the progress they make. Success flourishes with passion, hard work, support, and opportunity. Essentially, though, achievement begins with a goal.

Most people do not plan to fail, they fail to plan. - John Beckley

The skill of goal setting is essential to progress. Learning music requires students to plan and to set short and long-term goals. These goals should be explicit and conscious. People sometimes fail to succeed because their goal setting is unrealistic. If we set goals that are much higher than we have previously achieved we set ourselves up for failure. Conversely if we keep our sights too low we never will improve substantially enough to enjoy the fruits of increasing achievement. Lack of proficiency is a primary reason people give up music, and this is often related to poor goal setting.

There is an old saying "Life is too short to do what I have to do; it's barely long enough to do what I want to do." One should set genuine goals. This means the goal is your goal; an expression of what you genuinely want to achieve. Ask yourself, *is this something I really want to do? Will I enjoy it, and am I likely to continue to do so in the foreseeable future?* People sometimes choose goals based on what they think they *should* do. They choose goals based upon society's definitions of success and achievement. Young adults succumb to the pressure of what parents, teachers, peers, or significant others think they should do. If your goals are not congruent with your personal desire, then the pursuit and even the achievement of these goals might take you further away from what you truly seek. Self-determination requires not only self-perception, but also the ability to resist the social pressures that lead you off course.

Setting goals is a great way to fill the mind with positive thoughts. Goals are motivational; goals inspire! What counts is that your goal matters greatly to *you* and provides *you* with a set of challenges to overcome. Long-term goals, such as becoming a musician or learning a complex piece of music, need to be broken down into mini goals. This is what the next chapter on musical practice explores.

Chapter Two

How to Practise

When children practise music they usually play straight through a piece without stopping to correct mistakes. Correction attempts, if any, are usually superficial and ineffectual. As children become metacognitive, they learn to identify errors and engage in the deliberate practice strategies of repetition, chunking, and slow play. *Deliberate practice* is not only confined to the development of expertise in music but also appears in sports. Children who are unable to apply these learning strategies will lack progress. When individuals do not make progress they often give up trying.

Achieving high levels of musical expertise requires considerable practice. The figure of ten thousand hours to reach expertise in any domain puts the quantitative time requirement into perspective, and 'deliberate practice' describes the qualitative requirement. Experts know *how* to practise, not just how much. The efficient use of practice time requires intense and thoughtful practice techniques. The good news is there is nothing magical about being a successful 'practiser.' This is a learned skill.

All musicians get physically and mentally tired, but older children can practise longer than younger children. The amount one should practise depends on one's goal. Essentially one should practise as much as necessary to learn and stabilise a targeted passage. If, at the next practice session, errors are apparent then one should again target these passages. Learning requires patience because it takes as long as it takes. Effective practice methods result in effective learning. So sure of this was American educational psychologist Barry Zimmerman that he performed a fascinating experiment. Zimmerman wanted to examine whether the way people described their practice habits could predict their actual ability. Hence, Zimmerman did not observe actual skills but examined the way the players spoke about their practice methods. Working with a multilevel group of volleyball players, Zimmerman accurately predicted skill level 90 percent of the time (17).

One of the first questions a parent asks is: "When should my child start taking lessons?" Suzuki Method creator Shin'ichi Suzuki recommended that musical training start from birth, in line with language learning (18). During a child's infancy parents should provide a stimulating environment to encourage musical exploration and curiosity. For most infants musical learning is incidental in nature, in the form of vocal prosody (the emotional/musical aspect of the voice) and the pitches and rhythms in the surrounding environment. When early-childhood music lessons begin they should be fun and informal, in the company of a warm and friendly teacher. During this stage brains are most malleable and training can be very effective. When children display curiosity and fascination they are ready and willing to begin formal instruction. In the Suzuki method this usually begins at about the age of four, depending on the child's overall development.

To become an exceptional adult musician almost certainly requires an early start because of the time requirement, particularly for physically demanding instruments such as the piano and violin. Starting young can also set in motion a number of motivational conditions that lead to outstanding achievement. Take the case of Johnny, who is studying Grade Five violin at age nine, when most children at this level are several years older. Due to his age, Johnny will receive more praise, encouragement, and recognition than the others. People will think it is remarkable that he already is playing at the level of older children, even though it is not all that remarkable because it can be explained logically. Johnny has practised about the same number of hours as the older children who are playing at Grade Five level but, because of his age, people will tell him he is a special boy and lucky to have this wonderful gift. Having started young has provided Johnny with an opportunity to accumulate more hours of practice and therefore make more progress. This will result in his receiving more attention from adults, which will fuel his desire for attention and praise. Johnny loves playing the violin and in time might develop his own intrinsic motivation. At this stage of his development, however, the recognition, attention, and feeling of specialness provide powerful motivation for him to practise.

Should parents force their children to practise? On the one hand, parental pressure can destroy a child's sense of motivation: if the child takes the initiative, it is best not to interfere. On the other hand, commitment is fundamental to character. Commitment perseveres through low times and high times and helps individuals overcome difficulties. Children only can learn about commitment by being committed. As children grow, they learn about responsibilities, such as the requirement to complete school homework and the expectation to assist with household chores. Just as parents and teachers sometimes must encourage children with these obligations, so it is with music. The expectation of a commitment underpins the regard attributed to an activity. If there are household expectations in some areas, but not regarding music practice, it could imply to the child that music learning is not that important. Children always will be tempted to neglect their practice responsibility, just as with any other commitment. There were times in my childhood when my mother vehemently threatened courses of action if I refused to get back into a practice routine. The most effective of these was when she threatened to sell the piano. "Very well," she said. "We're selling the piano. It's just taking up space!" I'm not sure what other threat would have worked, but this one caused some serious thinking on my part. You cannot learn to play the piano without one, so did I really want to learn or not?

Having an explicit long-term commitment is a key indicator of future progress. In one study, children were asked how long they thought they might persist with learning their instrument. The options ranged from 'just this year' to 'throughout my whole life.' Responses were then categorised as short, medium, or long-term commitments, and practice patterns were measured. The finding was that children with the *idea* that music learning was a lifelong commitment were practising, and hence progressing significantly better than the other children. Even with the same amount of practice, the long-term commitment group was far ahead of the others (19).

Teachers should find opportunities to involve parents in their child's musical life. In general, parental involvement in children's educations results in positive outcomes. Improvements in school attendance, behaviour, the standard of schoolwork, and self-esteem all have been linked to parental involvement. Adult supervision and parental encouragement are crucial in the early formation of musicians. Children need models, not critics. In the home, parents do not need to understand formal music in order to watch the clock, detect wrong notes, and determine an appropriate tempo. Verbal encouragement, attendance at concerts and performances, and learning with the child all contribute in building enthusiasm. My mother listened to my practice sessions as she did the ironing. She guided me with simple comments regarding dynamics, tempo, mistakes, and the need for separate handwork. Parental guidance gives the immediate feedback essential for progress. My mother also engaged me using phrases including: "You've almost mastered this piece. Play my favourite for me. The neighbour is ill, offer up the next piece for her." Looking back I can see my mother used every ruse she knew to keep me practising. Supervision during practice is vital for beginners. As students become more mature and seek greater independence, supervision might become detrimental to the autonomy and intrinsic motivation of the student. At this stage, family musical support might take the form of attending concerts together, forming a family ensemble, or listening to music together.

Practice is more effective when it is systematic, structured, goal orientated, and thoughtful. Deliberate practice requires considerable effort and concentration. The teacher should model practice skills during lessons, rather than just talk through what needs to be done. Eventually students must learn how to learn, and learn to work on their own. The sooner young musicians become their own best critics, the less likely they will be shocked and disheartened at the judgement of external adjudicators. Signs of emerging metacognition include students setting practice goals, monitoring practice duration, using a metronome, composing music, and resisting distraction.

Some teachers write instructions in a practice diary. This is useful until the student has developed the metacognition required to determine his or her own practice methods, which may not occur until early adulthood. The child should be involved in maintaining the practice diary and can at least do the writing. Investment of personal effort is motivating; receiving instructions is not. "What shall we set for practice this week?" Questions such as this prompt the child to reflect on his or her learning and to take ownership of what is required for improvement. Furthermore, there are alternative ways of recording information to the traditional paper practice diary, such as video and audio functions built into mobile phones. Useful information might include teacher recordings of stylistic particulars such as phrasing, dynamics, and tempo.

One of the frustrations with attempting to learn any new skill is the rate of change of progress. With some instruments the initial period of learning a new skill is quick, and progress is clearly evident. Over time, as the rate of skill advancement is measured, signs of progress may become less clear. More practice may yield little additional improvement, which may lead to frustration. An explanation of this learning curve gives students reassurance that this is natural and not indicative of a lack of musical advancement on their part.

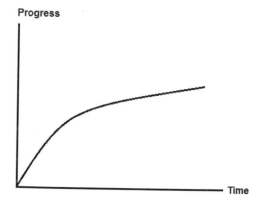

Figure 2: Progress over Time

Distributing Practice Over Time

"Sir, when should I practise? Practise only on the days that you eat."
- Shin'ichi Suzuki

Memory is more effective when learning is distributed over a period of time rather than in one hit. This process of memory consolidation is known as the *spacing effect* and was first recognized more than a century ago. [9] The benefits of the *spacing* effect apply to so-called 'muscle memory' as well as cognitive memory. Hence, musicians should practise regularly for shorter periods (distributed practice) rather than less regularly for longer periods (massed practice). For example, one hour per day for six days a week is more effective than six hours one day per week, and two forty-five-minute sessions per day is more effective than one ninety-minute session.

Massed practice, like cramming, might be effective for tomorrow's examination or performance, but a considerable memory loss occurs over the days and weeks that follow. Memory formation takes time to make the transition from short-term recall to long-term memory. Pioneering psychologist William James considered cramming a poor way to study and incongruent with how the brain functions:

> Cramming seeks to stamp things in by intense application immediately before the ordeal. But a thing thus learned can form but few associations. On the other hand, the same thing recurring on different days, in different contexts, read, recited on, referred to again and again, related to other things and reviewed, gets well-wrought into the mental structure. This is the reason why you should enforce on your pupils habits of continuous application. There is no moral turpitude in cramming. It would be the best and the most economical mode of study if it led to the results desired. But it does not (20).

---

9   You can find more information in the book *Memory: A Contribution to Experimental Psychology* (1885), by German psychologist Hermann Ebbinghaus.

Distributed practice is more successful for the longer term because between each practice session, what has been learned is forgotten at least partially, and must be retrieved. Paradoxically, forgetting is the friend of learning. Forgetting requires relearning, which sets memories more securely. The more times we are required to retrieve or generate answers, the stronger the neural circuitry of the learning becomes. Therefore rest times between practice sessions are not only important for mental regeneration but also to engage us in the 'forget and retrieve' process. The efficiency of distributed practice means that students should need less total practice time to achieve the same long-term learning results as those yielded by massed practice. Similarly, within a given practice session, passages can be targeted in a blocked or spaced manner.

Blocked and Spaced Repetition Within a Rehearsal

Recently I was watching television when a commercial break interrupted my program. Commercials are annoying at best, but this set of five commercial spots really got under my skin. This is because one of the commercials played *three* times, not in a row, but with a different commercial in between. Just when I had forgotten it, back it came to haunt me. And I thought rondo form was just a musical concept!

A	B	A	C	A

The repeated commercial A was deliberately interspersed with other commercials. The arrangement was cleverly designed to make me forget and retrieve, and I found it difficult to dislodge the commercial from my attention for some time afterward. I had to acknowledge that this marketing technique was really successful. I had 'learned' the commercial. Maybe I can turn this irritant to my advantage.

German psychologist Hermann Ebbinghaus famously revealed the *forgetting curve,* proposing that students forget 90 percent of what they learn within thirty days. Further to this disheartening finding, the most significant memory loss occurs within the first hour. A memory becomes more robust when the information is repeated in timed inter-vals. The more repetition cycles, the better for learning, and the more spaces between the repetitions, better again.

Imagine you have thirty minutes available for practice and have decided on three passages on which to work. How would you distribute this amount of time? You could practise the target passages in three blocks consecutively.

Passage A—ten minutes
Passage B—ten minutes
Passage C—ten minutes

Or you could practise them in the following manner.

Passage A—four minutes
Passage B—three minutes
Passage A—three minutes
Passage C—four minutes
Passage B—five minutes
Passage A—three minutes
Passage C—six minutes
Passage B—two minutes

The first method is referred to as *blocked repetition*. The second, like the television commercial example, is known as *spaced repetition*. Blocked rep-etition refers to sticking to a single practice task until it is effectively learned then progressing to the next learning task. Spaced repetition switches between different tasks during the course of a single practice session. In both methods one encounters the same material for the same amount of overall time, but as with the distributed practice concept, spacing the repe-titions exposes one to learning the task repeatedly over a longer time span.

Blocked repetition is a useful technique for introducing new skills to create a foundation. It is effective for beginners as it allows them to concentrate on a single task. Even for advanced musicians, very difficult passages require a single focus and attention that might be disrupted if one switches frequently between tasks. However, blocked repetition requires the intense engagement of the learner. If concentration wanes during blocked repetition, progress can stagnate and possibly deteriorate. It is essential to remain attentive and fully alert during practice.

Provided that the practice time is not restricted, and that the learner has the metacognitive ability to determine practice goals, spaced repetition is more effective than blocked repetition. Varying practice tasks frequently creates interference, which leads to a degree of forgetting. As with distributed practice, the benefits of spaced repetition relate to stronger memory formation due to the principle of forgetting and retrieving. When one revisits learning material a neural reconstruction takes place leaving a deeper impression on the brain. Spaced repetition can be frustrating because it involves more frequent failure and more mental effort, but the rewards are worth this extra effort. Marketing teams and musical learners use spaced repetition, as do professional athletes. For example, golfers are required to play shots of varying distances. Whereas blocked repetition drills require a golfer to hit many consecutive balls to one distance marker before practising another distance, spaced repetition alternates distance, replicating the real demands on the golf course. On one occasion at the British Open Championship I witnessed Tiger Woods practise in this manner. In skill-based endeavours, drills can provide an illusion of competence. Most teachers have heard their students say, "But I could play it yesterday!"

Spaced repetition can work in concert with blocked repetition, so music teachers should model how a practice session might alternate between the two. Practice technique also should be modelled to students in ensemble rehearsals. In any given rehearsal, I aim to revisit the passages that require the most attention at least three times throughout the rehearsal. I answer initial squawks from students ("But we've already practised that piece!") by explaining the rationale behind spaced repetition. Teachers cannot expect students to integrate these learning concepts if they do not exhibit them in their own methodology. I have known some music students to successfully apply the principles of spaced repetition to other school tasks. Students love to learn how to learn better.

The Learning Power of Repetition

We are what we repeatedly do; excellence, then, is not an act but a habit. - Aristotle

Repetition is the fundamental requirement when one is developing the complex muscle movements required in music and sports. Nothing is as important as the quantity and quality of repetition. Performing virtuosic music demands some of the most complicated motor patterns possible. At very fast tempos the execution of notes occurs faster than the performer can think about them. The process of repetition enables these complex motor actions to become automated which in turn frees up the brain to concentrate on other considerations such as interpretation. Automation enables performance with less conscious effort and greater accuracy.

Physiologist Homer Smith cites skilled piano playing as one of the pinnacles of human achievement because of the "demanding muscle coordination of the fingers, which require a precise execution of fast and complex physical movements" (21). This remarkable human ability provides an insight into the power of the brain. Consider Frédéric Chopin's popular but challenging *Fantaisie-Impromptu*. This work requires playing approximately nineteen notes per second. The performer must learn these notes to such an extent that conscious attention to them is virtually no longer necessary. This is the aim of any playing of music—to render the technical demand to an almost unconscious level. Daniel Levitin says, "Plain old memorization is what musicians do when they learn the muscle movements in order to play a particular piece" (10). Much of this repetitive practice routine is more or less an algorithmic task. There is nothing particularly creative about learning the motor mechanics of a phrase; if you repeat an action in a certain manner and for a sustained period of time, the brain faithfully will learn, and the muscles will obey.

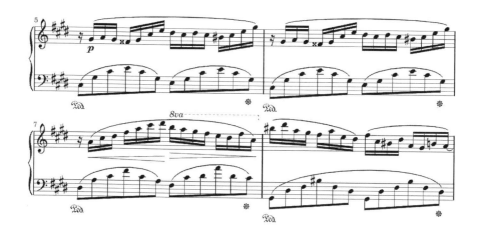

Figure 3: Chopin *Fantaisie-Impromptu*, Measures Five to Eight

Now that one has mastered the muscle movements, the focus shifts to expression. Consideration of tempo, dynamics, tenuto, articulation, and phrasing all combine to transform the notes into music. This is conscious and cognitive. With the focus now on musical expression, the playing becomes less mechanical. Miles Davis said, "The notes I do not play are more important than the ones I do". A musician who concentrates on mechanics alone cannot be a master.

I don't mean to underestimate the physical demands of playing nineteen notes per second on the piano. Each finger requires at least two vertical movements as well as lateral ones. Each finger movement involves all three joints, and even motionless fingers are tensed, ready for action. Performing approximately 380 distinct motor actions per second, a skilled pianist can do all of this and still focus on the musicality of the work. This muscle count is calculated before we even get started on other muscular systems in the hands, arms, and shoulders. Further, each note must be timed and executed with an individual's interpretative judgment, and when notes are played simultaneously, the fingers must differentiate volume levels for acoustic mixing of treble and bass, sometimes accentuating an inner melody. As if this were not enough, *Fantaisie-Impromptu* requires the mastering of polyrhythmic demands, meaning two rhythms occur simultaneously. Almost every bar requires the right hand to play sixteen notes against the left-hand twelve. This is a far cry from 'Rub your tummy while patting your head.' *Fantaisie-Impromptu* is difficult but not as fearsome as some works in the literature of piano music. More complicated works have passages that require up to thirty notes or about six hundred muscle movements, per second, although this does seem to be the upper limit for muscle coordination. When it comes to complex muscle coordination, musicians – not footballers are the super athletes of the world!

Achieving a stage of unconscious competence is necessary because the storage capacity of the unconscious mind is much greater than that of the conscious mind. According to Daniel Coyle, the unconscious mind can process eleven million pieces of information per second, but the conscious mind is limited to about forty (12). One achieves unconscious competence in only one way: by repeated practice. It is a wonder that humans have the capacity to learn all these muscular micro-movements with such accuracy yet still manage to express themselves musically.

The inflexible and automatic knowledge gained through repetition is the foundation of expert performance, but you have now been warned— repeat carefully! The learning brain does not distinguish between good and poor habits but learns whatever we repeat. Repetition creates permanence, and habits are difficult to correct. In particular pay attention to rhythmic accuracy. Rhythmic patterns are robustly set in the memory and difficult to alter once in place.

Inexperienced learners struggle with the discipline required for repetition and get lulled into a false sense of mastery when they judge themselves as having played a passage reasonably well. Without sufficient repetition, however, the learning soon will unravel. Teachers should practise in front of students, modelling the 'how' of repetition. It is advisable to give young musicians who have not yet reached the metacognitive stage a quantifiable number of repetitions to aim for in their practice, perhaps a number not less than six. As students become more mature learners they regulate repetition, depending on the complexity of the passage. Experts repeat short passages of music again and again.

Most musicians stop repeating when they play a passage correctly, but it is crucial that they keep repeating *after* this point. Brain connections strengthen and consolidate with myelin, a substance that insulates the axon of a neuron; it is known as the white matter of the brain. Myelin development seems to be a key for learning and maintaining skills because it increases the speed and accuracy of data transmission. Myelin formation is more important than the number of neurons in the brain. Albert Einstein's brain, for example, had no more neurons than the average brain, but it had twice as much myelin. Experts have more myelin build-up on the neural circuits pertinent to their domain than do non-experts. In 2005 a Swedish professor found a positive correlation between myelin development and the number of hours professional pianists practised (22). Myelin is a product of activity and is one aspect of *brain plasticity*, a term that refers to physical changes in the brain. Brain plasticity includes an increase in myelination and an increase in the number of connections between neurons. In musical learning, increasing repetition of a phrase after one plays it correctly builds myelin, which supports consistent and accurate performance.

> *The amateur practises until he gets it right. The professional practises until he cannot get it wrong. - Stephen Hillier*

> *The amateur stops repeating when he gets it right. The professional repeats well after to consolidate the myelin coating of the axon sheath. - Michael Griffin*

It is common to confuse temporary performance effects with long-term learning. The teacher or parent may mistake the phrase "But I played it better yesterday" as a white lie, and the student might be disillusioned because he or she thinks the blocks of repetition should have been sufficient for more permanent learning. There are two issues here. First, even with spaced repetition the consolidation pro-cess takes as long as it takes, and then some more for good measure. We cannot predict how much repetition it will take to master a skill but human nature almost always underestimates this. If a passage a student thought he or she learned yesterday is a muddle today the student must repeat the repetition process. Try not to be despon-dent. This is a natural part of acquiring skill. Memories do not just form at the point of learning so it may take several sittings for neu-ral connections to become strong. Some people seem to learn more quickly than others, but learning is not a race, and we are all capable of complex skill development through repetition. It may take one per-son six hundred repetitions over two weeks to consolidate a phrase, while it may take someone else only three hundred repetitions in one week. Students must learn to be patient and trust in the power of repetition.

Repetitio est mater studiorum! [10]

Second, you must know how to repeat. For many students, repeti-tion leads to boredom and loss of attention. Spaced repetition will increase alertness, but repetition also needs variation. Variable repe-tition maintains the essential nature of the exercise, as it incorporates small changes in tempo, dynamics, and articulation. This requires more conscious engagement on the part of the learner, but repeat-ing material in a variety of ways builds thicker, stronger, and more hardwired connections in the brain. Teachers in all subjects special-ise in designing learning experiences based on variable repetition. In chapter six I discuss the benefits of using songs to assist learning in mathematics and foreign languages. I also use songs to reinforce the principles of deliberate practice. Singing a *learning song* is another form of variable repetition. The words can be a little quirky or even silly, which will add to the multisensory fun that enhances enjoyable learning.

---

10 Latin proverb, "Repetition is the Mother of Learning."

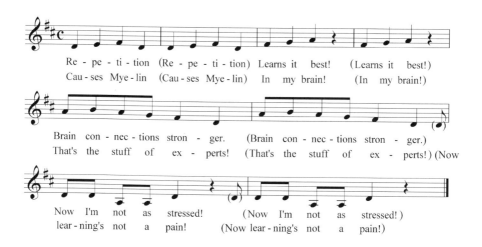

Figure 4: The Repetition Song
Words by Michael Griffin

Have a Rest

When you have done your musical day's work and feel tired, do not exert yourself further. It is better to rest than to work without pleasure and vigour. - Robert Schumann [11]

University of Texas Professor of Music Robert Duke and his team sought to determine the potential benefits of resting during music practice (23). Could having a rest during practice improve learning? One experiment involved three groups of learners practising a simple motor-skill sequence for the same length of time. One group rested for five minutes early in the practice session; another group rested comparatively later in the practice session; and the third group practised without taking a break. The researchers found a significant difference in performance improvement among the groups; the group that performed the best was the one that rested early in the practice session. According to Duke, early rest breaks are effective, because "Early breaks during the initial phases of motor sequence learning

11 Advice to Young Musicians, http://www.gutenberg.org/files/28219/28219-h/28219-h.htm.

allow time for the neuro-physical processes that underlie consolidation to engage, and after extended intervals of rest early in initial training sessions, the encoding of new procedural memories is in some way advantaged" (23). For this to occur, one must practise enough to establish a neural representation of new memory. Then the conscious imagination or subconscious psyche can continue to repeat the learned motor drills.

Although this type of research is interesting, it is still in its infancy, so we must be cautious not to over-interpret the results. The experiment involved simple motor-sequence skills one could master in a brief time. There is no evidence that this concept applies to more complex learning or over longer time frames. This experiment supports the theory that neural processes are strengthened during breaks and thus improve skill performance, but the interesting revelation is that early, rather than later, rest improves performance. This idea is new.

Sleep Learning

Sleep well, think well. - John Medina (88)

Since the year 2000 Matthew Walker, now with U.C. Berkeley's Sleep and Neuroimaging Laboratory, has been conducting experiments to determine whether humans consolidate learning during sleep (24). In one study, two groups of subjects practised a typing task using their left hands. The groups practised in the morning and were tested for improvement eight hours later. During the day, one group took a nap of about seventy-five minutes while the other stayed awake. For the group that remained awake the test found no significant increase in skill, whereas the group that took a nap recorded a significant increase. NASA also found that having an afternoon nap increases pilot performance. Is there merit in structuring daytime naps after a session of music practice? Have I finally found justification for my afternoon nap? Bliss! [12]

---

12   Ericsson's study of graduating violinists at the Music Academy of West Berlin found that the highest achievers took more afternoon naps and slept more at night.

A different study involved testing pianists to learn a short melody. Subjects in Group A were trained at 10:00 a.m. and tested again at 10:00 p.m. They did not sleep during this time, and no significant improvement in performance was noted. Subjects in Group B were trained at 10:00 p.m. and tested again at 10:00 a.m., following a night of sleep. Performance improved significantly (25). Many scientific studies reinforce the importance of sleep. When players on a Stanford University basketball team increased their sleep time, the team's over-all competitive performance improved (26).

Sleeping seems to do something to improve memory consolidation that being awake does not. Sleep and rest studies confirm that memo-ries do not just form at the point of learning and that the learning brain does not cease activity when practice ends, whether one is asleep or awake. Neural circuitry takes time to form and consolidate and may require sleep before one recognises the full benefit of practising. This knowledge should alleviate some of the frustration students feel when they do not observe immediate improvement after practice. It also reinforces the importance of getting things right in the first place, prior to rest or sleep. In other words, do not practise mistakes.

> *We should look at sleep as an active process. Getting enough sleep is a positive thing, which will help you perform in all aspects of life. It may be that extra sleep leads to more effective training routines and helps us learn patterns better.*
> *- Derk-Jan Dijk, Professor of Sleep and Physiology at the University of Surrey*

Chunking

You have ten seconds to memorise and reproduce this list of words.

black, flat, criminal, division, table, dog, lawyer, long, little

This is difficult. Why? One might say 1) "I need more time to engage in repetition to learn this"; 2) "The words are not connected. They have no real meaning"; or 3) "My mind cannot hold this many items on the fly."

All three responses are valid. Now let's rearrange the words.

little black dog   flat table   criminal lawyer   long division

In this example, we find connections between words and convert them into phrases. Hence we have reduced the learning load from nine items to four. Previously the phrase 'little black dog' was three separate, unconnected words, but now it is one item because the words relate contextually. This concept is called *chunking*. Chunking recognises that we can hold only a limited number of items in our short-term memory. Chunking allows us to recognise patterns in order to reduce the cognitive load.

Cognitive psychologist George Miller introduced the term 'chunking' in a 1956 paper. [13] Miller found that short-term memory could handle between five and nine discretely different pieces of information only, at any given moment. [14] Chunking increases short-term memory capacity by recoding information. In the exercise above, we connected related words to make short phrases. We use chunking when we learn and convey telephone numbers by joining digits together for easier recall. Reading is a form of chunking. Paragraphs, sentences, and punctuation break up information into small units because the reader can absorb only a certain amount of information in a single try. We see words and then sentences rather than individual letters, even if the letters are out of order. *You wulod not blveiee how mcuh my msiuc pcartcie has iorpmevrd!* Acronyms, abbreviations, and mnemonics are all chunking devices because they make remembering easier by assisting short-term memory.

---

13   Miller, G. 1956. "The Magical Number Seven, Plus or Minus Two: Some Limits on Our Capacity for Processing Information." *The Psychological Review* 63:81–97.
14   For most people this number is closer to five, six or seven.

Some root knowledge is important for chunking. One cannot relate 'criminal' and 'lawyer' without knowing that a relationship exists between these words. In music theory, being able to find connections lessens the requirements of memory. Take key signatures as an example.

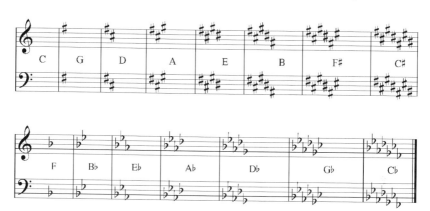

Figure 5: Major Key Signatures

The majority of young musicians are comfortable with a knowledge of key signatures up to a couple of sharps and flats only, and struggle to recall more difficult key signatures. Observing a simple connection between the sharp and flat keys of the same alphabetic letter name provides an almost instantaneous solution to remembering the more complex key signatures. Perhaps you can see this connection. Look at the sharp key and the flat key for the letter G. G-major has one sharp. G-flat major has how many flats? Repeat the exercise with another pair of alphabetic letter names such as B major and B-flat major. [15] You will find that the sum of the sharp and flat keys for the same letter name is seven. Noticing this simple connection provides a solution to recalling key signatures. Chunking is the secret ingredient for memory feats. Experts are great chunkers; they discover patterns to simplify their learning.

The limitation of short-term memory capacity invites us to learn more thoroughly in smaller portions. It also explains the value of

---

15 This procedure uses the concept of simultaneous equations to find a formula.

making many of our actions automatic so we can focus on other things. Successful musicians isolate short phrases for rigorous attention. They de-construct key ideas into small bits and practise them repeatedly in a variety of ways. Elements which can be isolated include rhythm, articulation, and technical difficulties such as hand movements on a piano. In music practice we learn small chunks that gradually become larger until we can memorise long passages of music. Musical notes become phrases, which in turn become sections, then movements. Once the short-term memory converts to long-term memory, there seems to be no limit to how much the brain can store. [16] Chunking is appropriate for musical learning because music is based on repetition and pattern. Do not be put off by the jungle of notes on the page, as the chunking process reveals there is less on that page than meets the eye.

Take the first movement of Mozart's *Sonata in C, K545*. Measures five through eight are modes of a C-major scale, immediately apparent to the trained eye. A friend once asked me, "How do you remember so many notes?" Musicians do not see notes individually. By chunking we see phrases, and this C-major scale passage is bread and butter to us. Music is filled with patterns such as these.

Figure 6: Mozart Sonata in C, K545, First Movement, Measures Five to Eight

---

16 I have heard estimates of the data storage capacity of the human brain being anywhere from 4 terabytes to 1 million petabytes.

Somewhat more advanced is the arpeggio section: measures eighteen through twenty-one. This passage conforms to the ubiquitous chord progression represented by the scale degrees '14736251' in the key of G-major. Jazz players in particular will recognise this, thereby reducing these four measures into one chunk of information.

Figure 7: Mozart Sonata in C, K545, First Movement, Measures Eighteen to Twenty-One

Understanding the formal structure of a piece is another form of chunking. For example, musicians who understand rondo form (ABACA) and are able to recognize it in, say, *Für Elise,* will have the advantage of a cognitive map to work with when attempting to play from memory. In this example chunking reduces five sections of music to three.

The power of words and concepts helps us to chunk more effectively. Students are sometimes slow to understand that the purpose of musical theory is to simplify their learning, not to add burden. Theoretical knowledge facilitates the identification of musical patterns such as scales, arpeggios, and sequences for the purpose of chunking. The greater the familiarity and technical proficiency with these patterns, the easier it will be to understand and perform the demands of the piece.

If you are a teacher, you can use the following song to reinforce chunking with students.

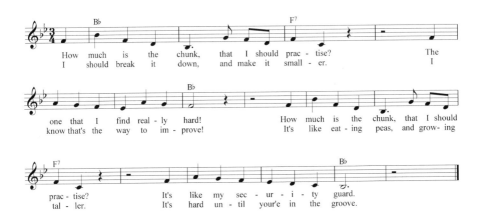

Figure 8: The Chunking Song
Words by Michael Griffin

Slow Practice

Maintaining improvement and making a skill permanent require slow steady work that probably forms new connections.
- Norman Doidge (27)

Sergei Rachmaninoff said, "The most efficient manner in learning to memorise a piece seems to be the one which proceeds in an error-free manner." He believed that if musicians avoid mistakes during practice, chances are that they will avoid them in performance. Rachmaninoff was known for his excruciatingly slow practice. He used a metronome on the slowest tempo and moved it in small increments for successive repetitions.

The concept of slow practice can be difficult for children to grasp. Interpretation of 'slow' varies considerably, and children's interpretation, as a whole, is definitely faster than that of adults. For many children the ultimate aim is to play music quickly. In their minds increasing the tempo indicates progress, so it seems a retrograde step to slow it down. Teachers must explain why slow practice is effective and necessary. Then they should model what a slow tempo sounds like and have their students copy them at that tempo. Simply telling students to "practise this slowly at home" is ineffective. Gary McPherson says, "Teachers rarely provide demonstrations of how to use a strategy, perhaps because they assume that their pupils will learn strategies merely on the basis of verbal instruction" (28).

Tell me and I forget.
Show me and I remember.
Let me do and I understand.
- Confucius

Slow practice is crucial even if we can play accurately at faster tempos, because the brain prefers slow learning to strengthen and myelinate neural connections. Daniel Coyle states, "Neural circuits do not care how fast you go. What matters is that they fire consistently and accurately." Coyle cites an example of the Meadowmount School of Music in New York State where a teacher tells students, "If your practice is recognisable to a listener then you are playing it too quickly" (12). Meadowmount School aims for a 500 percent increase in learning speed and a central precept in achieving this is slow practice. Mozart used a practice routine that combined chunking, repetition, and slow playing. In the form of a game he placed ten dried peas in his left coat pocket. After each successful attempt at mastering a phrase he shifted a pea to his right coat pocket. After ten successful repetitions Mozart allowed himself to proceed to the next phrase, but if he made a mistake he had to start all over again. You can imagine the slowing down and the attention to detail as his repetitions progressed.

As unlearning is more difficult than learning it is best to play a piece correctly early before flawed habits lodge themselves in the brain. A quality process will deliver a quality result. This is the QIQO principle—quality in, quality out. [17] Learning something new requires building a neural circuit, and this is best done slowly. As the English proverb states, "An ounce of prevention saves a pound of cure." Hungarian composer and pianist Stephen Heller said, "Practise very slowly, progress very fast." Practise slowly to get things right as soon as possible.

---

17 This is in opposition to the GIGO principle—garbage in, garbage out.

Figure 9: The Slow Song
Words by Michael Griffin

Figure 10: The Too Fast Song
Words by Michael Griffin

Teachers should incorporate repetition, chunking, and slow practice into ensemble rehearsals. Not surprisingly the less accomplished ensembles disregard these principles. Children accept the failure of an ensemble as their fault when in truth the director carries most of the responsibility. Managing an ensemble presents an opportunity to model practising techniques. In my choral workshops I model and explain repetition, chunking, and slow practice to observers. When one is learning a new skill, learning models rather than technical experts often make the best teachers.

New teachers are susceptible to over-teaching. They fall into the trap of providing excess verbal instruction at the expense of offering a simple model. Sometimes it is better for teachers to keep words to a minimum and allow students to copy them. It is important for students to engage in experiential learning; teachers do not always need to intellectualise the lesson. Searching for improved tennis training methods, Tim Gallwey did exactly this. He experimented with nonverbal instruction, asking his pupils to observe and copy him. His experiment was an unqualified success. Gallwey states, "I was beginning to learn what all good pros and students of tennis must learn—that images are better than words, showing better than telling, too much instruction worse than none" (29).

I once had a nonverbal teaching experience in China when presenting a jazz choir workshop for about 250 delegates. I was misled into believing that they could speak English. As my words were useless, all I could do was model, gesture, and invite a response. It was a great learning experience, and the delegates did not run away either!

Endeavouring never to perform a mistake is a noble aim but we all experience nervousness, loss of concentration, and self-doubt. When mistakes occur one should correct them as soon as possible after the performance. When performing at the Burj al Arab Hotel in Dubai I kept a notepad with me to record problem areas that required further attention. I do not like musical mistakes incubating in my brain so after each performance I returned to my hotel room and practised. Learning solidifies between practice sessions so problems must be attended to before the passage of time reinforces errors.

Observing Others

Students must practise how to practise, but first they need a model from whom to learn. How many students have the opportunity to watch their teacher practise, and how many teachers observe their students as they practise? We learn a great deal from observing others. On my first visit to New York City I had hoped to attend a concert featuring Chick Corea, Bobby McFerrin, and the New York Philharmonic, but it was sold out. Fortunately the rehearsal was open to the public. Witnessing one of the world's great orchestras in rehearsal was a priceless experience, more valuable to me than attending the actual concert. During a school choir tour to Europe in 2003, a highlight for my students was witnessing the Vienna Philharmonic Orchestra rehearse Mahler. Students need to witness a new level of excellence to reset their goals. When I wanted to raise the bar with the Brighton Secondary School Stage Band in Adelaide, Australia, I had them workshop with the university big band. Purposeful listening is a crucial activity for all musicians. Observing a practice session is valuable, and opportunities abound to do so for free or at least inexpensively.

Live concerts inspire and motivate children. When I was a boy my mother took me to see Australian pianist Roger Woodward at the Adelaide Town Hall. It was my first real concert, and everything about it impressed me: the at-capacity audience, their earnest appreciation for the music, and the beautiful square marbled hall. I was in awe of the passion, the beauty, the emotional intensity of Beethoven's sonatas, and the virtuosity of Woodward's pianism. The audience response was overt and joyful; it conveyed to me that something important and vital had just taken place. The significance, gravity, and intensity of the entire event captured me, and from that experience I wanted to play Beethoven's music. This was a crystallizing experience in my musical childhood. Another early crystallizing experience occurred at a distant relative's birthday party where an elderly man played an old upright piano. My mother was astute in finding opportunities to inspire me musically, and she promptly introduced me to Don, asking him if I could watch him play. His wonderful music amazed me. Don was not a music reader but improvised and played by ear. I wanted to be like Don and have the same freedom from notation in my playing. Don, however, impressed upon me that he wished that he could read music, and he encouraged me to continue to develop my music-reading skills. I came away with the view that reading music and being able to play without music are both important. One never knows when the arrow of inspiration might strike. Parents and teachers must set up numerous opportunities in the hope that they might capture a child's curiosity.

Music competitions and festivals offer opportunities for students to listen to others. Implicit in the nature of competition is the impetus to be evaluative, to compare, and to make judgements. These higher-order thinking skills are essential for personal progress. To turn competition into a real learning experience, teachers can assign students a project to evaluate ensembles based on criteria pertinent to the genre. In a choir competition, I would ask students to comment on the following:

- Is the singing in tune?
- How well are the parts balanced?
- Can I understand the words? Is the text uniformly articulated?
- Is there sufficient word-painting or emphasis on important words?
- Is the emotional intention of the piece being conveyed?
- Are the dynamics appropriate and sufficiently contrasting?
- How engaged is the choir with this song?
- How engaged/interactive is the conductor with the choir?
- What is noticeable about the posture of the choir?
- Does the choir work as one at the beginning and end of phrases?
- Do the ends of phrases finish accurately?
- Is the piano accompaniment balanced with the choir?
- What do I like about this performance?
- What would I do differently?

Expression

Fluent and error-free playing is essential for an enjoyable musical experience, but the emotional character of the music is what makes for a striking performance. This non-verbal characteristic gives music its *raison d'être*. Emotional expression and reception are innate. We observe this when a mother speaks to her infant who, incapable of understanding the words of language, can respond only to the prosody, the musical and emotional characteristics of the human voice. Lullabies—slow, soft, and mostly of major tonality—are uttered for sleeping and calming, and short, sharp, and agitated phrases for correcting. Emotion in music, as in speech, is meaningful. The musician who can capture and communicate an authentic emotional experience will win the hearts and minds of an audience.

The ability to be musically expressive increases as technique develops, but significantly each of us has a unique set of feelings and emotions upon which to draw. This is our advantage: to be uniquely expressive. Musicians must get in touch with their emotional reactions to music and fuse them with the intended emotional character of the composition. When a musician internalises, synthesises, and expresses this, magic takes place.

Teachers can encourage expressive playing by relating the inner world of the performer to the objective features of a performance. As a training exercise, students can play scales and exercises with an emotional quality and in so doing learn to associate appropriate musical attributes with emotion—for example, conveying *anger* through the use of loud volume, short articulation, and appropriate tempo. Use the list of emotional descriptors in Figure 30 for ideas. Imagery is a potent means of improving the expressive aspects of performance. When a performer creates an internal emotional state he or she will enhance the emotional qualities of the performance. As a boy I played Khachaturian's *Toccata in E-Flat Minor*. I was not exactly sure what the composer had in mind when he composed this, but my mother painted a landscape of Russian tanks forging through a bleak and harsh winter, and this image helped me connect with the gravity and grimness of the piece. This enabled me to convey meaning, and the music became more enjoyable to play. Another way to help students with expression is through modelling, as I have indicated in reference to other aspects of teaching and learning. Observational learning allows students to experience emotional performances free from the demands of performance. Musicians learn from listening to, watching, discussing, and copying others. Along with teacher and peer observation, YouTube, that ever-growing repository of music performances, provides worthwhile opportunities for modelling. YouTube's numerous interpretations of repertoire provide opportunities for compare-contrast assignments, which engage learners in analysis and reflection of emotional interpretation. Here is a sample assignment for students.

Find three versions of (your piece) on YouTube.

1. Describe the expressive differences in each.
2. How does the performer achieve the desired emotional expression?
3. Which version do you like the most and why?

Active and Passive Leisure

I did not wish to find when I came to die that I had not lived.
- Henry David Thoreau

You are lying on your deathbed. Any regrets? A commonly expressed regret is not having engaged in sufficient active recreation. Learning a musical instrument; joining a choir; establishing better relationships; and participating in scuba, golf, art, drama, or writing are some of the activities people would like to have spent more time pursuing. The least common responses include spending more hours at the office, reading more gossip magazines, and watching more television. Television, however, gets the lion's share of our precious leisure time.

Relying on external means for happiness is hopeless. - Dalai Lama

Generations of adults spend years participating in inactive leisure pursuits that dull the senses at the expense of learning and applying skills. Ken Robinson's distinction between leisure and true recreation compares the "effortless and passive nature of leisure with the re-creating action of recreation" (30). Just as physical and mental effort energizes recreation too much passive leisure can be draining. Our consumerist and commercial media lobby on behalf of Passive Entertainment, Incorporated. They beguile us to seek happiness through external means, proposing that satisfaction and happiness need little personal investment except our cash. Children need a counterbalance. Parents and teachers must educate them regarding the benefits of personal action and involvement in activities such as music and sports, in contrast to the dangers of being inactive. Kahlil Gibran writes about this in his 1923 philosophical classic *The Prophet*.

> Or have you only comfort, and the lust for comfort, that stealthy thing that enters the house a guest, and becomes a host, and then a master?
>
> Ay, and it becomes a tamer, and with hook and scourge makes puppets of your larger desires.
> Though its hands are silken, its heart is of iron.
> It lulls you to sleep only to stand by your bed and jeer at the dignity of the flesh.
> Verily the lust for comfort murders the passion of the soul, and then walks grinning in the funeral.

The systematic time investment required for musical progress can be stolen by time thieves, and television is one of the great offenders. After work and sleep, television consumes most of our time and attention. On average, people watch three hours per day. For most people, this is half of their available leisure time and amounts to ten years spent in front of the television in an eighty-year lifespan. People who watch television feel relaxed and passive. When they turn off the television, however, the sense of relaxation ends, but feelings of sluggishness continue. "The television has absorbed viewers' energy," says Mihaly Csikszentmihalyi, "leaving them fatigued, disheartened, and after large quantities of viewing, slightly depressed" (31). People also report having more difficulty concentrating after watching television.

I find television very educational. Every time someone switches it on, I go into another room and read a good book. - Groucho Marx

For children, television is a wonderful multimedia art form capable of educating and amusing us. The problem lies in the vast number of hours people spend watching it; television viewing can turn into an addiction. When watching television interferes with the ability and desire to learn new things, to participate in real life, and to commit to music practice, there is clearly a problem. Excess television viewing acts as a parasite of the mind. Not only does it dull the mind, but it also steals time from our lives, including precious music-practice time.

Children who choose to stop watching television show an improvement in concentration and mood and behave better in school. They also become more involved in activities such as music, sports, and reading (32).

It is in the improvident use of leisure that the greatest wastes of life occur. - Robert Park, American sociologist

Television is not the only time thief. In one Australian study, eighty percent of secondary school students reported distraction and procrastination due to the time they spend on Facebook (33). Some older teens are recognizing the problem, and desperate for productivity, are asking friends to change their Facebook passwords for them, locking them out of the site. Other students are activating temporary website-blocking programs such as SelfControl. Not only are the students frustrated, but also educators and teachers at major institutions such as Harvard and MIT are becoming increasingly exasperated with their students' distraction from being constantly online (34). Harvard Law School's Jonathan Zittrain labeled the phenomenon 'demoralizing,' and the University of Chicago turned off wireless networks in classrooms. Some educators believe the present generation of teenagers will adapt to multitasking but a 2009 Stanford University study found that this is unlikely.

Multi-taskers make more mistakes. They are distracted more easily, have poorer concentration, work less efficiently, and do not write as well (35).

Attending to e-mail, inseparable in many people's business and social organisations, is another time thief. An Australian investigation found that "Workers spend on average 14.5 hours per week checking, reading, deleting, arranging, and responding to e-mail" (36).

The future will belong not only to the educated, but to those educated to use leisure wisely. - Charles K. Brightbill

Computer games are more interactive than watching television, but the creative aspect is mostly reactive and responsive rather than self-initiated. This is because most computer games generate play content that must be followed. A Carnegie-Mellon study found that by the time a boy turns twenty-one he is likely to have spent about ten thousand hours playing computer games. This is the same amount of time the average student spends in school from the fifth grade to twelfth grade. This is also the same amount of time required to develop an expertise.

Including television, computer games, and social networking sites, children aged eight to eighteen spend approximately 6.75 hours per day in front of a screen (37). What is the return on this time investment? Success requires time. In my workshops I have students conduct an inventory of their time usage. Not only do they analyze where their time goes, but they also commit to shifting some of that time to more important activities, such as music practice. Children often are amazed at where they spend time and how unrelated it is to their life goals. A time inventory can provide the necessary wake-up call.

This can be a matter of balance. We all need to wind down. To relax and just *be* is important. We are, after all, human beings, not human *doings*, but if passive leisure is the single object of recreation, its pursuit can become meaningless. The effects of passive leisure are ephemeral, but recreation has meaning for the long-term. It is surprising that with so many opportunities for recreation and leisure, enjoyment can be elusive. Studies show that many people find more meaning and happiness at work than in their leisure time. To really enjoy leisure time, some active challenge is necessary.

Stephen Covey makes the distinction between urgency and importance. He demonstrates that for many people urgency dominates their lives to the point that they never get around to doing what is important. The graphic below makes this concept clearer.

	Urgent	Not urgent
Important	**1** Pressing issues Crises Deadlines	**2** Preparation Plannning Personal development
Not important	**3** Interruptions Some emails	**4** Time wasters Trivia Excessive television

Figure 11: Time Management Matrix, Adapted from
***First Things First*, Stephen Covey, p. 37**

Many of the best things in life, including learning music, fall into quadrant two, but because they are not urgent, they do not get done. Naturally, quadrant one must take priority. If there is a fire in the music room it is classified as urgent and important and must be attended to immediately. Most people live in quadrant three and confuse urgency with importance. To achieve meaningful goals we must adjust our time management. Time management is not just about the quantitative but also about spending time in quality engagement that leads to productive outcomes. Advances in technology and modernism are designed to create more time for quadrant two, but many of us still flounder in quadrant three.

> *Fatigue does not come from working hard, but from leaving tasks incomplete. - William James*

The movie *Dead Poets Society*, with its life-force statement 'Carpe diem,' offers a powerful message for teenagers. Robin Williams's character, Mr. Keating, emboldens students to think independently, to be wary of conformist pressure, and to use their precious leisure time to "suck the marrow out of life."

Robert Herrick's poem "To the Virgins, to Make Much of Time" appears in the film and underscores its message of the importance of seizing the day.

> GATHER ye rosebuds while ye may,
> Old time is still a-flying:
> And this same flower that smiles to-day
> To-morrow will be dying.
>
> The glorious lamp of heaven, the sun,
> The higher he's a-getting,
> The sooner will his race be run,
> And nearer he's to setting.
> That age is best which is the first,
> When youth and blood are warmer;
> But being spent, the worse and worst
> Times still succeed the former.
>
> Then be not coy, but use your time,
> And while ye may go marry:
> For having lost but once your prime
> You may forever tarry.

Let us encourage today's children to make the most of life, to resist the enticement of indolence, and to commit to achieving goals in their chosen fields.

Performance Stress

The heart is pumping—thump, thump, and thump! You shake, perspire, breathe quickly, and swallow the little saliva that remains. What can this mean? Only that you are about to play in front of an audience.

When I was a boy, I once performed Franz Liszt's *Consolation No. 3 in Db*, a piece that requires constant use of the pedal. Out of nowhere, out of control, and for the entire piece, my right foot shook, tapping the pedal more violently than Thumper's paw in *Bambi*. I did not welcome this out-of-time percussion accompaniment. Not everyone suffers this way, but nervous adrenaline is powerful. Ignore it at your peril!

Stress is the perception that a given challenge is greater than the abilities we possess. This perception might not be real or accurate. We all fight with negative thoughts from time to time; disappointments from the past but mostly concern regarding our future performance. To put this in perspective I invite students to recall times when they were stressed about a test but achieved better-than-expected results. Students then realise that stress can be self-induced.

Man is disturbed not by things but by the views he takes of them.
- Epictetus

The attitude we bring to a challenge determines whether stress will have a positive or a negative bearing on our performance. Imagine two golfers are facing the same shot. The aim is to strike the ball straight down the middle of the fairway. On the left is an out-of-bounds fence, which adds pressure to the shot. One golfer thinks in terms of negative outcomes. *Do not hit it left; it is out of bounds and will incur a penalty. It will ruin my score if I hit the ball left. Do not hit it left*. This focus on negative outcomes usually brings about one of two negative results. The first is the self-fulfilling prophecy: it is likely the golfer will hit the ball left, as this is a focus of his thoughts. Second, the shot might go in the other direction, far to the right of the target area. In psychology this is known as overcompensation. The other golfer, however, sends his brain a different message and a singular one. This golfer observes the fence on the left but thinking *I will hit the ball down the middle of the fairway*. Focusing on a positive outcome will more likely deliver a positive result. Stress is useful if we can harness it to narrow attention on successful outcomes, but destructive if it leads to a focus onto negative outcomes. Stressful situations are such that the same amount of pressure will wilt one person and invigorate another. Losers visualise the penalties of failure and potential humiliation; winners visualise the rewards of success and welcome the accompanying learning experience. Stress impedes concentration and is an enemy of memory. It tends to make the emotional limbic part of the brain, which controls our 'fight or flight' responses, dominant. Physical responses to stress include an increase in pulse rate (which can cause the tempo of a piece of music to increase), body temperature (which results in sweating), and blood pressure; a dry mouth; shortness of breath; and tension in the form of muscle contraction. [18] Unfortunately these outcomes are detrimental to the physical control required for vocal and instrumental performance. Understanding the physiological responses to stress and having realistic expectations of what might transpire can be effective in helping to place the experience in perspective.

Physical responses to performance anxiety are symptomatic of thought processes. Musicians with a fixed-intelligence mindset worry more about audience perception than do musicians possessing a growth-intelligence mindset. The fixed-intelligence mindset person thinks, *If my performance is poor, the audience will think I'm not as gifted as I'm said to be*. A fear of making mistakes hinders performance. Perfectionists often have a fixed-intelligence mindset. They have such an aversion to making mistakes that they focus more on what's wrong that what's right. The unrealistic expectations of perfectionists can lead to lack of enjoyment as well as low self-esteem. Performance is less stressful for the growth-intelligence-mindset person. *I have prepared well,* he or she may think. *No one likes making mistakes, but if that happens, I will learn from the experience, find out what went wrong, and work harder.*

---

18 Not to mention rapid foot movement.

Fear causes one to want to flee from a situation. In her book *Feel the Fear and Do it Anyway,* Susan Jeffers encourages readers to confront their fears rather than allow fears to hold them back from living life to the fullest. The only way to get rid of the fear of doing something is to go out and do it. Therefore the way to get used to stressful situations is to place oneself in stressful situations, meaning students should seek performance opportunities rather than avoid them. There is no substitute for concert experience, where one can encounter nerves and learn how to deal with them. All musicians need performance practice. Recently I performed in Australia. I visited many friends on the tour, and if they had a piano I would ask to play for their children. I was out of concert practice and needed to take every opportunity I could find. As a pianist, there was the extra value of encountering a variety of pianos, each demanding a unique requirement of touch and tone generation. Students need to play often in front of different groups of people, and more useful still, in the presence of distractions or people who make them nervous. If it can be organised, have the student rehearse where the concert will be taking place.

Positive self-talk is one of the best methods for reducing doubt and anxiety, but it must be rooted in reality or the performer might falter at the first sign of trouble. Negative self-talk increases doubt and anxiety. A high degree of pessimistic self-talk is known as catastrophizing, which creates an imaginary doomed outcome, such as *I know I'm going to crash in the cadenza!* Once you start to worry about correct notes and fluency the result can be a disaster. It takes practice to change our thought processes. Once a performance begins, to avoid worrying about hypothetical trouble spots or mistakes, we must stay in the present. This is more difficult than it seems as 'now' means about three seconds. When we stay in the present we think less, which includes less worrying and fearing, and trying too hard. Constant thinking activity interferes with procedural skills. One way of staying in the present and curtailing a wandering mind is to sing the melody in your head as you play.

> *Do not dwell in the past; do not dream of the future. Concentrate the mind on the present moment. - Buddha*

Optimal performance requires a stillness of the mind. When we perform at our best there seems to be a certain unconscious element. We are in 'the zone' and it just seems to happen. The unconscious mind becomes one with the body, and there is a flow-like merging of action and awareness. Once we start to think about what we are doing, however, we lose the magic. Sometimes trying too hard induces poor outcomes. In the art of effortless concentration there is no room to think of the 'how-to' aspect. With an ironic sense of detachment we must trust that our deliberate practice has formed the skills necessary for a successful performance. Relax, and let it happen. Try not to worry what the audience may be thinking. The focus must be away from the self and the ego. This is not as easy as it seems; it takes practice to still the mind and to keep invading thoughts on a leash. Some musicians turn to yoga, listening to music, deep-breathing exercises, or other meditative practices to achieve this.

In performance try not to give mistakes your attention. Frowning and other facial expressions do not aid in concentration, nor do they assist in physical execution. Rather they create a tension that constricts the muscular action required for fluid performance. It is natural to be driven by a desire to succeed, and accepting that mistakes and failure are part of the human journey creates a less stressful perspective of purpose. Experts thrive with a consistent purpose, but experts also accept that mistakes are part of the improvement process. Learning must include a certain amount of failure. Perhaps musicians can learn from golfers. The game of golf is based on managing errors. Golfers know that if they stew over a poor shot and poor shots are inevitable it could affect the remainder of their game. The late and great Spaniard Seve Ballesteros took an 'instant amnesia' approach to mistakes while on the course. He only attended to his mistakes at the appropriate time, and that was after the round.

It is impossible to sustain consistent success by chance, so solid preparation is the only preparation. The pressure of public scrutiny will expose any weakness. Expert performers prepare better than others. Students must continue to practise pieces they already have memorised and know well. They can achieve this by playing slowly and by beginning at different restart points within the music. Mental rehearsals leading up to the performance should visualise and auralize success.

CHAPTER THREE

THE SOFT SKILLS OF ACHIEVEMENT

I have discussed how musical attainment will advance as a result of the quantity and quality of practice time. Achievement in any domain, however, requires another set of core skills. Why are some people motivated to work harder and longer? How do they ignore distractions? How can teachers instil a mindset of determination, perseverance, and self-discipline in students? I call these qualities the soft skills of expertise. First and foremost we must find motivation.

Motivation

> *Nothing great was ever achieved without enthusiasm.*
> *- Ralph Waldo Emerson*

Motivation is the fuel of human behaviour. It creates a desire to persist beyond the boundaries of comfort, to overcome obstacles, and to achieve beyond our own, and others', highest expectations. Motivation is highly valued because it gets results, so it must be an overarching concern for parents and educators. In general terms, motivation is categorised as either intrinsic or extrinsic.

When we enjoy an activity for what it is and for the pleasure it brings, we are self-motivated; also referred to as 'intrinsically motivated.'

The reward for doing the activity comes from the activity itself. With extrinsic motivation the reward is an external benefit pertaining to the activity. We observe intrinsic motivation when students engage in activities alone, when they choose to participate in activities without external pressure, and when they engage in activities in the absence of the promise or opportunity for external reward. It is not only the choice to engage in activity that defines intrinsic motivation, but also the quality of that involvement. With music, does the student attend to difficult passages thoroughly or just go through the motions? Trying hard and spending extra time on a task are examples of intensity and persistence. These are hallmarks of an intrinsically motivated student.

Extrinsic motivation is entrenched in schools and education. External rewards—including gold stars, stickers, and grades—are both material and verbal and presented with the hope that students will be encouraged to learn. External motivation tends to be transient in that students are likely to lose their motivation when the potential for external reward disappears. Extrinsic performance goals and intrinsic learning goals are different. Getting an A in music class is an extrinsically motivated performance goal, whereas becoming a better musician is a learning goal. This is one of the drawbacks of grading systems. Students are interested in achieving good grades but become less interested in learning as a result of being graded. When students focus on grades they do the work that is necessary to get that grade but rarely more. In comparison to learning goals, outcomes from performance goals are shallow and limited. Also, striving for good grades can lead to overly conformist behaviour as students try to please the teachers who are grading them.

Intrinsic interest is a natural disposition that is more likely to result in sustained motivation over a longer period. Have you ever seen an infant who was not curious and self-directed? We are born this way, with an inherent tendency to seek out novelty and challenge, to exercise our abilities, and to explore. Extrinsic rewards can deliver short-term boosts but the effect wears off and can reduce longer-term motivation. Offering a reward conveys a message that the task is not inherently enjoyable, beneficial or valuable. This form of encouragement coaxes with contingent promises of positive (or negative) consequences. Daniel Pink says, "Pay your son to take out the trash and you've pretty much guaranteed he will never do it again for free" (38). Once you offer a reward for undertaking an activity there is no going back. I suspect my parents realised this when they raised us. My siblings and I received a little pocket money but in no way was this connected to the expectation that we help with household chores.

In the book *Punished by Rewards,* Alfie Kohn says that children who are driven by extrinsic motivators never develop the natural curiosity and desire for self-fulfillment required to engage in deep learning. Kohn argues that aside from failing to motivate, contingent rewards "kill creativity, undermine interest, fail to alter the attitudes behind learning behavior, and rupture relationships" (39). Contingent rewards are based on performance outcomes, namely, 'If you do this, I will give you that.' Harvard Business School's Teresa Amabile found that rewards can be particularly detrimental in regard to creative tasks:

> Managers in successful, creative organizations rarely offer specific extrinsic rewards for particular outcomes. However, they freely and generously recognize creative work by individuals and teams—often before the ultimate commercial impact of those efforts is known (40).

Any extrinsic reward should be unexpected and offered only after the task is complete. Celebrating after the outcome does not undermine learning because it recognizes something that was competently achieved. This eliminates the 'if.../then...' condition to act. However, there is an exception to this rule where the offer of a contingent reward might be appropriate. Some enjoyable activities demand an initial effort that may not be naturally enjoyable and therefore might require incentives to initiate the first stage of learning. This is sometimes the case when very young children are coming to terms with the peculiar technical demands of an instrument.

Intrinsic motivation is clearly linked with higher quality learning. Therefore a central mission for teachers and parents is to foster conditions so that children become intrinsically motivated. If this happens, children more than likely will give their best and reach greater heights. The key model that has influenced more studies on motivation than any other comes from the work of two psychology professors at the University of Rochester. Since the early 1970s, Edward Deci and Richard Ryan have tested and refined ideas about motivation, which has resulted in what is known as Self-Determination Theory (SDT).

This theory is based on three innate human needs: the need to belong, the need to feel competent, and the need to direct one's own actions.

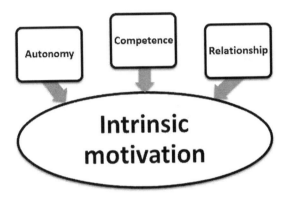

Figure 12: Deci and Ryan's Model for Intrinsic Motivation (Self-Determination Theory)

Autonomy

We are most engaged and do our best work when we act according to our own will. - Richard Ryan

Autonomy refers to actions chosen and endorsed by the actor. The key here is *choice*. By increasing students' options and choices, teachers improve the conditions for intrinsic motivation to occur. As early as possible, teachers should give students some control of their learning. Coercion can cause students to learn reluctantly, but self-direction and choice are motivating. Choice might be as simple as involving students in selecting repertoire. With access to so much wonderful music teachers can offer choices that fulfil the required technical and aesthetic goals. The enjoyment factor of learning music is paramount. Students should be involved in decision-making processes as often as possible. In general, in education, children have too little choice regarding what they learn. In the book *Overschooled but Undereducated: How the crisis in education is jeopardizing our adolescents,* UK educator John Abbott says that children have no choice in approximately 75 percent of school learning activities. Children are always requesting to do things their own way, and they do not like being forced to conform any more than adults do.

In 2010 I had the pleasure of speaking to a group of students at Eton College in England. The Parry Society, named after eminent British composer and Etonian Hubert Parry (think *Jerusalem*), is an organisation of senior Eton music scholars and masters. I was particularly impressed that the boys organised every aspect of my visit, including all correspondence, setting the date of my visit, arranging transportation, and attending to my presentation requirements. As their director of music, Ralph Allwood, said, "I do not really have a say in it. The boys make the choices and organise everything themselves." The boys even choose their guest speakers.

Autonomy also refers to an internal *locus of control*. That is, to what effect can *my* actions and *my* effort determine future outcomes? The alternative to this is an external locus of control. Attribution theory asks the question "Why am I good at what I do?" For musicians the question might be "Why am I good at music?" Let's look at three possible responses.

1. I was born this way. I got lucky in the genetic lottery and have a special innate musical gift.
2. I have a really good teacher. In fact my teacher once told me, "I will make you a fine musician."
3. I work at it. I practise hard, I seek advice, and I learn from my mistakes. My effort is the primary reason for my progress.

The first two responses attribute competency to factors outside of the self. This mindset undermines autonomy which in turn undermines intrinsic motivation. The third response supports autonomy and an internal locus of control. This is the growth-intelligence mindset that fosters the positive learning behaviours discussed in chapter one.[19]

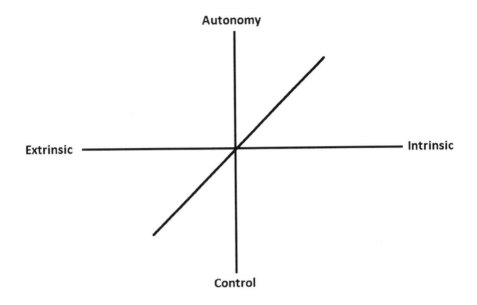

Figure 13: Autonomy and Control

Control can include contingent rewards and some types of verbal feedback. The functional significance of feedback is dependent upon the perception of the student. Feedback that is informational and related to competence is motivational, but feedback that is perceived as coercive or controlling of behaviour undermines motivation. For example "Your dynamic contrast between themes was striking" is informational feedback whereas "I really like it when you sit quietly and don't talk" will be perceived as an attempt to coerce behaviour. Successful learners have the presence of mind to seek feedback; quality feedback is essential for progress in any field. It allows us to redefine our goals and stay on course to reach these goals. Teachers should give feedback that is

---

19 See the work of Carol Dweck in her book *Mindset: The New Psychology of Success.*

consistent and accurate, and they should give it quickly and frequently. Feedback that is provided too readily, however, might deter learners from processing their own self-evaluation. Be careful with praise. Tim Gallwey says, "Compliments are criticisms in disguise because both are used to manipulate behaviour" (29). This reasoning implies, *if he likes me for doing well, he might dislike me for not doing well*. Praise and criticism are part of the same continuum of judgement.

It is important to identify what is being praised and why it is being praised. If an activity makes children happy they do not need teachers or parents to tell them they did well. As with tangible rewards, there is a danger that children will shift the intention of their actions to the praise rather than to the activity. Children will comply with the wishes of parents or teachers because they are hungry for approval. Helpful praise describes what is observed. The comment, "Your dynamic contrast between themes was striking", refers to an important attribute of a performance. "Your hard work and attention to detail have resulted in a commanding performance" praises effort and process. This type of praise is essential in fostering a growth-intelligence mindset. A useful technique is to frame praise within a question: "How did you manage to play through that entire passage without any mistakes or hesitations?" Parents and teachers must think through their motives in saying what they say and then consider how to phrase their words so children do not interpret it as an evaluation. *Sticks and stones may break my bones but words can cause irreparable damage.*

Boys' education expert Ian Lillicoe recommends praising a boy through touch, such as giving him a pat on the back. [20] This can be critical for alienated boys, because touch is often missing at home. In many societies a sense of touch has been lost, and society has become paranoid about it, but boys connect with one another in a very physical way. In one Australian state, after several years of enforcing a 'no touch' policy in schools, legislation was introduced that allowed a pat on the back for building rapport and as a non-verbal form of praise.

---

20 See http://www.boysforward.com.au.

Albert Einstein was sceptical about the merits of praise, saying, "The only way to escape the personal corruption of praise is to go on working." Extrinsic motivators can destroy intrinsic motivation; the two coexist uncomfortably.

> *Two kinds of motivation are not better than one. Extrinsic will always erode intrinsic. - Alfie Kohn, 'Punished by Rewards'*

Relationship

Intrinsic motivation is more likely to flourish when the student feels connected with the teacher. Strategies for enhancing relatedness include conveying friendliness, concern, and respect for the student.

> *They don't care how much you know until they know how much you care.*
> *- anonymous*

Students need to know that teachers genuinely like, respect, and value them. When students connect with and respect their teacher, they are more likely to subscribe to the values and practices of that teacher. If the student does not like the teacher very often they will not do well in that subject. Some evidence suggests this is particularly true for boys. If girls like a subject, even if not the teacher, they are more likely to prevail.

> *Boys learn teachers. Boys will work hard for a teacher they like.*
> *- Steve Biddulph, 'Raising Boys'*

Working in groups gives students the opportunity to enhance relationships with their peers. As a twelve-year-old student in Dubai said to me, "It is very good fun to learn with my friends." Learning within a social environment is natural and good fun.

Recognition

Public performance encourages extra practice because students find the prospect of transmitting aesthetic excitement to other people stimulating. The recognition that follows performance is one of the strongest motivating and influential forces for musicians. Inherent in public performance is a relationship between the musician and the listener. The listener shows interest in the musician's display and expresses appreciation with applause and verbal feedback. This recognition provides feedback regarding the musician's competence and boosts self-esteem.

Teachers must find opportunities for student performances. Studio teachers can have students perform for one another on either side of their lesson time. Students can also perform for one another in group lessons. Facilitating students to perform for younger students offers many benefits. I have students perform for younger classes and remind them of their influence in being positive role models to children younger than themselves. This sentiment is genuine; the performer feels important and valued, and the audience will be generous in response. Younger students are eagerly inspired by their seniors.

I remember an occasion when I asked fifteen-year-old Daniel to play electric guitar at the primary school assembly. Daniel was nervous and told me he could only play a brief repetitive riff. He was not keen to perform. During the performance nerves got the better of Daniel and he played well below his potential. Looking disappointed, Daniel trudged off the stage, albeit accompanied by huge cheers from the young audience, which, I suspect, was due to the guitar distortion and thunderous volume as much as anything else. I took the opportunity to call out to the audience in a loud voice, "Did you like that?" After the cry of "Yes," I responded, "Would you like to hear it again?" Reluctantly Daniel got up and played it a second time, and his performance was much better. Due to the forgiving nature of the audience and a little prompting we transformed Daniel's initial performance into a positive experience. After the concert Daniel brimmed with confidence and declared that he would practise more thoroughly so next time he could play an entire piece.

Another performance opportunity is the parent concert. When parents are included in their children's music activities, good things happen. Relationships improve between parent and child, parent and school, and child and school. From witnessing a school concert parents will more than likely become advocates for the music program. In the present educational climate advocacy for music education is necessary. School newsletters provide opportunities to promote course rationale, pedagogical method, and the latest neuroscientific research supporting music education, as well as the usual informational material. Most of society is not familiar with the depth, breadth, and value of music education. When I present music seminars in schools I suggest that the school program an after-hours time so that parents can be involved. Parents love to learn about successful practice methods just as much as teachers and students do, and inevitably they find the content fascinating and relevant to their personal learning experiences. Parents are grateful for the opportunity to be included in their children's education.

When Teresa Amabile was researching motivation factors among senior business executives she expected recognition to be the number-one motivational force. However, she found an even stronger motivation—the prospect of making progress. People love to get better at what they do.[21]

Competence

Humans have a fundamental need to feel competent. Self-efficacy is a person's belief in his or her own competence. For intrinsic motivation to flourish, however, feelings of competence must be accompanied by a sense of personal control.

---

21 *Harvard Business Review* offers numerous podcasts with Teresa Amabile and other business experts. These are available on iTunes.

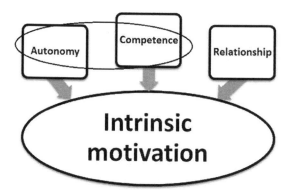

Figure 14: For intrinsic motivation to flourish, competence requires autonomy.

It is essential that teachers assist pupils to experience competence. Success results in personal pride and generates enthusiasm and perseverance. Perseverance is about finishing tasks and is at least as important for success as is intelligence. Success leads to further success because achievement is motivational. Many students judge their performance or success by the goals they achieve. Task goals, such as taking exams, lead to pride and satisfaction. Examination preparation can be motivating. One study found that 92 percent of students practised more when preparing for an exam than at other times throughout the year (41). Developing an increasing level of competence, or making progress, is a great motivator. Feelings of competence increase when one meets an optimal challenge. How does one identify such a challenge?

Optimal Challenge and Flow

'Flow' refers to an optimal state of awareness that occurs when a person is intensely focussed, deep in concentration, and fully immersed in an activity (31). For flow to occur, one must engage in a challenge that requires the full use of one's skill. For example, a tennis match between closely matched opponents is likely to result in flow for both players because they test one another to the full extent of their ability. This creates a merging of awareness, action, and attention, and the individual becomes absorbed or lost in the present moment. The body and mind are stretched in a way that makes the effort rewarding and we emerge from the experience with a greater level of skill. Flow is the purest form of intrinsic motivation.

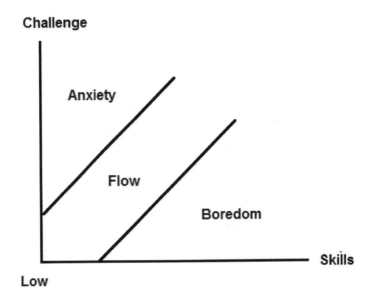

Figure 15: Adapted from *Flow*, Csikszentmihalyi, p. 74

To achieve flow the activity must have a level of challenge significant enough to increase skills, but it must also be in reach of present capability. Set the goal too low or too high, and we stray into the realm of boredom or anxiety. Once flow is achieved and we have acquired a newly developed skill level, it is maintained by again increasing the difficulty of the challenge. Being just out of our present grasp, this optimum learning zone involves effort. Working on the edge of ability, we push ourselves just beyond our present capability. Skill improvement requires struggle.

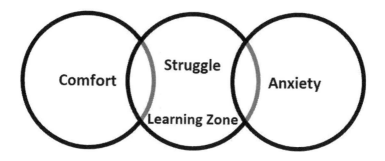

Figure 16: The Learning Zone

You do not get fit without some discomfort. Struggle and difficulty are essential to the learning process. The learner needs to focus on and analyse the issues required to overcome difficulties and problems. The young boy who can catch a ball at a distance of six feet will seek to increase the distance upon mastery of the present challenge. Effectively, he deliberately places himself back into a position of incompetence to create a new challenge. Flow experiences provide some of the best moments of life because they involve striving to accomplish something difficult and worthwhile. Making progress motivates one to keep seeking flow. Once the peak of flow is experienced, people invest extraordinary effort to repeat the experience. They become self-directed learners.

> *It is doubtful whether any heavier curse could be imposed on man than the complete gratification of all his wishes without effort on his part, leaving nothing for his hopes, desires, or struggles.*
> *- Samuel Smiles (1812–1904), Scottish author and reformer*

Expert learners seek the flow state. They deliberately direct, regulate, and reflect upon their learning in order to accomplish goals and increase their skills. I find flow when I practise the piano. Sometimes I get 'lost' in the activity and time seems to fly. I feel excited at the prospect of learning something new and improving my skills. In my life, I also experience flow through golf, scuba diving, presenting a seminar, and having an absorbing discussion.

The computer game industry now generates more money than the Hollywood film industry. One of the reasons these games hold such appeal is that they are designed around the powerful principles of flow. Computer games quickly determine a player's ideal level of challenge. When mastered, that challenge is increased incrementally. As the difficulty increases, so does the skill of the player.

When I was a boy I enjoyed playing table tennis with my father. Even though he was better than me, we managed to have competitive games. How so? Perhaps my father went easy, allowing me to win some points? No, even young boys have pride and I would not tolerate any suspicion that my father was throwing a game. My father played against me with his weaker hand. In this way we were more evenly matched and could fully use our skills to help each other to improve. The day arrived when my father reverted to his strong hand, which gave us more years of competitive table tennis. Flow experiences are created by manipulating the challenge and skills axes in Figure 15. In this example, my father deliberately reduced his skill level to create a better challenge for both of us. Competitive situations are a great way to achieve flow by creating the right amount of tension between challenge and skill. The best sporting contests are close games that provide optimal challenge. The Latin phrase 'con petire' ('to seek together') sums this up well; we seek to actualise one another's potential. Genuine joy in competition comes from the knowledge that we are getting better.

> Our antagonist strengthens our nerves and sharpens our skills.
> - Edmund Burke

I talk about flow in schools. Children love the concept and enjoy recounting their peak learning experiences. It might be basketball, orienteering, solving mathematical problems, playing music, or painting—in fact any activity that provides a challenge. The class soon learns that they can generate flow if they undertake the right challenge with the right attitude. When we learn music, to generate flow usually requires reducing the difficulty of the music. Chunking simplifies a musical challenge to a level more suited to our present skill level. We lower the challenge axis to match our skill level by isolating small passages for particular attention and also by slowing the tempo of our playing. This maintains the 'flow ratio' of skills to challenge and keeps practice manageable and enjoyable. But there are also times when we want to increase the level of challenge, such as when teachers need to engage more advanced students. In a piano lesson, for example, we might increase a challenge in any of the following ways:

- Play the melody with both hands.
- Play the melody with double octaves.
- Play the LH with the RH and vice versa.
- Dot-dash and dash-dot the rhythm.
- Change the meter.
- Change the key (play it in all keys).
- Change the tonality (major to minor, Dorian, and so on).
- Extend the melody with your own idea.
- Create a simple harmony for the melody.
- Choose more difficult repertoire.

Artificially increasing the difficulty of a challenge is common among experts. Professional golfers deliberately practise the hardest shots, and footballers try to kick goals from 'impossible' angles. No matter what the activity we can contrive to make it more difficult and create the conditions for flow. I once had a friend who worked in a bank as a teller. Joe found his job boring, so he invented ways to challenge his mind and keep mentally sharp. He did this by memorizing customers' names and account numbers. Joe got a buzz seeing the surprise on the face of a client when he not only knew his or her name but also could recite the client's account number.

At one time I was playing five to six nights per week as a resident musician, on Hayman Island Resort on the Great Barrier Reef in Queensland. Anyone who performs pop music regularly is used to enduring requests for the same song, night after night. This is not an issue for jazz musicians as original interpretation and improvisation are inherent to the style. But in the pop music world audiences usually expect an Elton John song, for example, to be played close to the cover version. To increase the challenge I would play the piece requested in different keys. Sometimes I practised the new key beforehand, but usually I launched into the new key, placing my skills and myself on the line. I was inspired by Adelaide pianist Denis, who aimed to play his pop repertoire in keys of not less than four sharps or flats. Denis and Joe are examples of autotelic, or self-goaled, personalities. Joe's quirkiness stimulated my thinking and Denis inspired me to challenge myself to reach greater levels of personal musicianship. Autotelic personalities constantly seek to challenge themselves to higher levels of understanding.

Enjoyment does not depend on what you do but how you do it.
- Mihaly Csikszentmihalyi

Autotelic learners do not wait for the teacher to set up learning opportunities but seek to learn in all manner of environments. When I was appointed conductor of an established and successful school choir, I prepared by watching rehearsals with the retiring conductor. This was an opportunity to learn from a conductor with more experience than me, and all it cost was a few hours of my time. The conductor was happy to mentor me, and I was sensible to accept. Learning opportunities abound, often free of cost.

There are other ways to contrive difficulty. When I was sixteen years old, I had a pep talk with Adelaide musician Bruce Raymond. My mother set up this meeting because she was worried that I was losing interest in the piano. Mum knew that Bruce, with whom my uncle had once worked, would be an effective model for me because at the time I was mad keen on Australian football. As well as being a top musician, Bruce was a football star, so I was all ears to his words. The first thing Bruce told me was that he practised the trumpet at 5:00 a.m. I responded, "Surely five a.m. must be the most difficult time of the day to practise a trumpet." This, Bruce replied, was precisely the reason he practised at this time. He believed if he could master his trumpet on chilly Adelaide winter mornings at 5:00 a.m., he would have the confidence to play at any time of day. Bruce's attitude inspired me. I learned to welcome the piano with stiff keys and Adelaide-morning-cold fingers, knowing these conditions only could make me stronger if I approached difficulty with the same attitude as did Bruce.

Autotelic personalities do not get bored because they keep redesigning their own learning, creating challenges for themselves in numerous areas of interest. Authentic education should result in students emerging with autotelic and lifelong-learning mindsets. A survey of 55,000 students at tertiary institutions in Australia and New Zealand conducted by the Australian Council for Educational Research showed that roughly 33 percent of students intended to drop out of their degree program. The number one reason was boredom (42). Given that available resources for self-learning and extension have never been greater, this reflects poorly on the quality of the students' education.

Flow in the Classroom

Flow is nurtured in a classroom or group context through *differentiation*, thereby allowing individuals to make progress at a rate that is appropriate to them. No one likes being deliberately kept behind in his or her learning or being forced to keep up with the pack.

The principles of differentiation are explicitly embedded in my general music course Music and Keyboard in the Classroom, which caters to classes of up to twenty-five students. [22] Its core pedagogical ideas include the following:

- All students are entitled to progress at their own rate.
- Self-evaluation precedes teacher evaluation.
- Skilful students earn the right to mentor and assess peers.

---

22 Contact the author or visit www.musiceducationworld.com for more details.

My research confirmed the appeal of this pedagogy.

- 95 percent stated they enjoyed the course.
- 97 percent stated they were satisfied with their rate of progress.
- 92 percent reported they enjoyed the opportunity to mentor their peers.
- 92 percent said they were comfortable with the incremental skill design.

Students appreciated being allowed to learn at their own pace.

> "I really like it (the course). I enjoy it because we each have our own levels, which means that if one person is behind we do not have to wait for them."

> "Everybody has their own levels, and it does not matter at all as long as you're happy with it."

Central to this course is a focus on learning practical musical skills. 'Rock Drum Patterns' is an example of a differentiated exercise. All students are capable of learning the first two-handed midi-keyboard drumbeat, but patterns two and three are more challenging.

Rock Drum Patterns

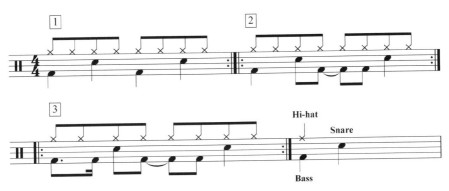

Figure 17: Excerpt from Music and Keyboard in the Classroom
By Michael Griffin

Self-Assessment

Self and peer-assessment is another core idea of Music and Keyboard in the Classroom. When assigned the piece 'Can Can' students are required to sign their work when they think they can play it correctly. This attempt must come before a teacher evaluation.

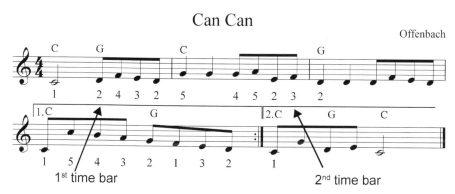

This piece has been played successfully.

Student signature.....................................

Teacher signature.....................................

Date.....................................

Figure 18: Excerpt from Music and Keyboard in the Classroom
By Michael Griffin

Some students will be reticent to self-assess and will want the teacher to evaluate for them. I've had students say, "You're the teacher. Just tell me what I have to do." But students must learn to assess their own levels of musicianship so that over time they will become knowledgeable and independent judges of musical excellence. This ability is crucial for developing autotelic learning. In cognition models, such as Bloom's taxonomy, the ability to self-assess is at the pinnacle of intelligent behaviour.

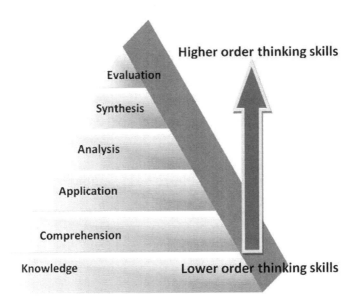

Figure 19: Higher-Order Thinking Skills Taxonomy, Bloom et al, 1956

Students must learn how to assess against set criteria. So they can practise this, I have them assess my playing, which includes examples of good, mediocre, and low performance standards. Students follow the score and evaluate my playing against criteria of correct notes, fluency, appropriate dynamics, and appropriate tempo.

The Inspired Student Teacher

In Figure 18, below 'Student signature' is 'Teacher signature.' This confirms the legitimacy of the student evaluation. It is essential that students receive feedback regarding their own evaluation progress, but this teacher verification does not actually need to be done by a teacher, per se. In my model 'teacher' includes student teachers. Why should adult teachers do all the evaluating? General music classes usually comprise students with a mixture of experience and ability, which creates opportunities to use student expertise. If students can play a particular exercise to a high enough standard I grant them teacher status for that exercise.

This is then indicated by placing 'T' in the box to the left of the signatures. In my model, student teachers have the authority to browse the class and assess others in the same way a real teacher does. Some ground rules help.

- Student teachers are to be respected and treated like regular teachers. Students who do not respect this process will not get an opportunity to become teachers.
- Student teachers may have their rights revoked if they are too lenient or too harsh when signing student work.

Students revel in the novel role that teaching offers and gain new insights into the learning and teaching process. One principle they learn is that teaching does not necessarily mean giving answers. This system creates opportunities for higher-level learning. It develops student leadership and responsibility and gives the classroom teacher time to monitor student interactions. I aim to give every student the opportunity to be a student teacher for at least one lesson.

Teaching is a powerful learning activity. Teaching enhances explanation skills and requires a deep understanding of the subject material. Verbal explanation develops deep understandings inherent in declarative knowledge.

How We Learn

10 percent of what we read
20 percent of what we hear
30 percent of what we see
50 percent of what we see and hear
70 percent of what is discussed with others
80 percent of what is experienced personally
95 percent of what we teach to someone else
   - William Glasser, American psychiatrist, born 1925

Like the quality of mercy, teaching is twice blessed. It exalts the giver and the receiver.

My student-teacher concept has been an unqualified success, and feedback from teachers around the world confirms its value. Likewise, 97.4 percent of the students I surveyed like the idea. Here is some of their feedback.

> "I like it because I can help other people!"
> "I enjoy that we can be 'teachers.'"
> "I enjoy that if you complete a piece well you can become a teacher."
> "I like being able to feel proud of myself when I pass a lesson or become a teacher."

The prospect of becoming a student teacher encourages students to engage in deeper levels of learning and practice. When teaching Music and Keyboard in the Classroom, I found that if student work had been successfully signed but the student hadn't reached teacher status, some students would stay with the exercise until they achieved the exacting standard required to become a student teacher. This splendid educational outcome also was found in a similar study involving college students, who were asked to learn science material for the purpose of either 1) teaching it to others; or 2) because they would be tested on it. Students learning with the expectation of teaching it to others developed a richer understanding of the material than those who learned for the test (43).

Enjoyment

> *Human beings seek self-esteem and happiness more than any-*
> *thing else. - Aristotle*

One of the clearest indicators of a motivated student is whether he or she enjoys the activity. It is natural to enjoy learning. We are all born eager to gain new knowledge of the world in which we live, and knowledge of ourselves. We observe this eagerness by catching a glimpse of a child's inspired inner world as he or she takes visible delight in learning something new. Motivated learners are curious. They want to explore further and ask a lot of questions. Enjoyment is more than an ephemeral feeling. It nourishes our brains and bodies and fosters better interpersonal relationships. Happy children pay more attention in the classroom. Happy learners learn better. Dale Carnegie said, "People rarely succeed unless they have fun in what they are doing." If students enjoy learning, they will develop a lifelong love of learning. Successful learning motivates because any increase in competency is accompanied by enjoyment and self-esteem.

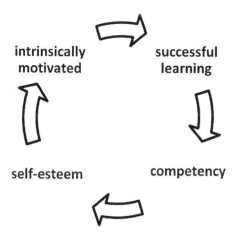

Figure 20: Successful Learning Model

The self-directed action of doing something for its inherent value, for the sake of self-growth, is characteristically exhilarating, gratifying, uplifting, and enjoyable. - David Elliott (44)

That most musicians are amateurs is evidence that making music is inherently enjoyable. Music teachers must help students recognise the enjoyment and satisfaction that come from the challenges of musical practice. When a student discovers enjoyment in learning, he or she will develop the ability to cope with the demands of work.

> *Whilst happiness is sought for its own sake, every other goal— health, beauty, money, or power—is valued only because we expect it will make us happy. Enjoyment is characterised by a sense of accomplishment. A person can feel pleasure without any effort, but it is impossible to enjoy an activity unless atten- tion is fully concentrated on that activity. The self does not grow as a consequence of pleasurable experiences.*
> *- Mihaly Csikszentmihalyi (31)*

Self-Discipline

> *If IQ was the biggest social construct of the twentieth century, then self-discipline is the biggest construct of the twenty-first century. - Stuart Shanker, York University, Toronto.*

In 1972 Professor Walter Mischel performed an experiment with four-year-old children. He wanted to see whether this age group could exercise self-regulation, and if so, whether a relationship existed between this ability and future life success. Each child was given a marshmallow and told that if they could refrain from eat- ing it for fifteen minutes they would get an additional marshmallow. Succumbing to temptation, two out of three children gobbled their marshmallow. Fifteen years later the children were re-examined. The children who had refrained from eating the marshmallow were more successful in life than those who had eaten the marshmallow.

> Children who are able to delay gratification are more popular, earn better grades, and had an average of 210 more points on their SAT tests.[23]

---

23 Shoda, Mischel, and Peake: The Stanford Marshmallow Experiment.

Another study, with grade-eight students, compared the roles of IQ and self-discipline in academic achievement. Self-discipline was found to be a substantially better predictor than IQ for successful academic achievement (45).

The ability to resist impulse is a soft skill of expertise. Our human weakness creates a continuous struggle and fight for control of our desires. We make annual resolutions to regain control of our lives, to be more financially responsible, to live more healthily, and to plan for the future. Our craving for immediate pleasures is evident in the thriving credit card industry. The need for instant gratification is the source of much debt and misery. Alternatively the ability to resist the impulse for immediate gratification pays a handsome dividend.

For a child the reward of becoming a competent musician can seem distant. Committed musical practice does not always bring satisfaction until sometime in the future. Therefore musicians must cultivate the ability to look further ahead than the present. Music learning is a prime example of a task that requires a regular and sustained effort for long-term incremental gains. With so many diversions competing for their attention, young learners must develop a capacity for singular focus. For one to achieve musical success, resisting impulse is essential. In his best-selling book *Emotional Intelligence*, Daniel Goleman writes "there is perhaps no psychological skill more important than resisting impulse" (46).

Attitude of Mind

> *The greatest discovery of my generation is that humans can alter their lives by altering their attitude of mind. If you change your mind, you can change your life. - William James (47)*

Attitude can determine the consequences of a predicament. Attitude alone can transform what seems to be a crisis into an opportunity. [24]

---

24 The Chinese character for "crisis" includes both danger and opportunity.

Teachers must help students find this inner resolve for those times when things get tough. They can do this by finding examples to which their students can relate.

1. Personal examples.
2. Peer examples.
3. Teacher/significant adult examples.
4. Historical-figure examples.

Persistence, when the going gets tough, is one of the most important indicators of long-term achievement. Teachers can encourage students to reflect on past experiences, recalling times when they persevered and overcame difficult circumstances. How did this feel? Was it worth it? Personal experience is a great educator. Putting students in touch with their resolution of past difficulties empowers them with the ability to overcome trying times in the future. Second to personal experience, the examples of peers are highly influential. Students often think, *If she can do this, then maybe I can too*. I comment upon the significance of peer example and influence in learning frequently in this book. Thirdly, the personal examples of significant adults, such as teachers and parents, guide and inspire children. Infused in the power of a story, anecdotes of adults' trials and tribulations and how they overcame them will captivate children. Finally, historical examples of courage and determination abound to inspire us all. Here are some examples.

Ludwig van Beethoven provides one of the most stirring examples of courage and fortitude in the face of personal disaster. The most renowned composer of his day—and perhaps of all time—Beethoven, in his mid-twenties, became aware of problems with his hearing. Over the next few years, and after many consultations with his doctors, it became clear that he was headed for a life without sound. Beethoven retreated to the country town of Heiligenstadt to reflect on his misfortune. Feeling hopeless, he even considered suicide. He wrote, "Such incidents drove me almost to despair; a little more of that and I would have ended me life." [25] But, reaching deep into his spirit, Beethoven resolved to continue living for his art. He changed his attitude and hence his life. "I will not endure this! I will seize fate by the throat," he proclaimed. "Most assuredly it shall not get me wholly down. I will struggle with this fate; it shall never drag me down."

Beethoven continued to compose, and his output during this difficult period includes some of the greatest music ever written. Some, such as symphonies three and five, are awe-inspiring in their depiction of triumph over adversity. Were these works personal testaments? Beethoven's fate would not rule his destiny, no matter how often it knocked at his door.

Winston Churchill was another who formed the ability to prosper in difficult situations. "When things are going well he is good, but when things are going badly he is superb!" said General Hastings Ismay, Churchill's chief military assistant.

Successful people overcome obstacles and even turn them to their advantage. Throughout his career Mozart battled illness, poverty, peer envy, a dominating father, and other setbacks. At the age of nine he suffered an illness that resulted in temporary blindness. Despite this impairment one might speculate that Mozart continued to practise and make best of his circumstance. We know one of his skills was to play blindfolded, or with his hands covered by a cloth, so perhaps the skill was honed during this illness. Likewise, when Mozart was eight and too ill to physically play music, he spent his time composing, which resulted in his first two symphonies. Persevering in the face of adversity builds character. Children, however, will not learn this if adults keep solving their problems for them.

Weakness of attitude becomes weakness of character. - Albert Einstein

---

25 Beethoven wrote a letter titled "The Heiligenstadt Testament" in October 1802. Beethoven stayed in Heiligenstadt, a suburb of Vienna, during the spring and autumn of that year.

Metacognition—A Coming of Age

To remain a pupil is to serve your teacher badly. - Friedrich Nietzsche

High on the mission statements of music teachers is to impart strategies that maximise musical success. In addition the ultimate objective for teachers is to become obsolete in the learning lives of their students.

Metacognition is that wonderful learning stage when the learner drives learning. An umbrella term, 'metacognition' means 'thinking about our thinking.' It includes self-reflection, self-knowledge about our learning skills, and self-evaluation. It involves understanding our motivations, setting goals, knowing which practice strategies to implement, and being able to exercise self-discipline.

Metacognition is the coming of age for a learner. It is the hallmark of intrinsic motivation.

Metacognitive learners take responsibility for their learning. Music students must be able to ask, "How effective is my practice? How effective is my learning? What do I need to do to get better? What practice strategy does this task require?" Successful analysis of problems gets to the heart of the matter quickly. Metacognition is not about factual knowledge or skill but the process involved in gaining that knowledge or skill. It enables us to question our beliefs and perspectives that colour our approach and attitude to learning. Children age eleven or twelve have an impressive body of factual knowledge but have comparatively low metacognitive skills. Metacognition usually flowers later, in adolescence or early adulthood, but it is a process dependent on the quality of teaching and parenting. Metacognition is a learned skill and one can nurture and enhance it with simple but powerful strategies.

Midway through my undergraduate music education degree I changed piano teachers. My first impression of new teacher Stephen was that he was strange. Stephen barely said a word, so how was I supposed to learn from him? When I played, rather than comment, he looked at me expectantly, as if he were waiting for *me* to do the analysis. Tolerating the silence no longer, I began to utter thoughts of my own. "Maybe this phrase could use more of a crescendo?" I'd ask. "OK," he'd say. "Try it." I would do so, and the process would be repeated. I might not have understood this at the time but Stephen was teaching me to think for myself, which led me into the world of metacognition. This was new. I was learning to teach myself. Prior to Stephen my experience with piano lessons was quite different. My role was as a passive receiver of teacher knowledge. My well-intentioned teachers always had given me directions and told me what I needed to do, and my job was to sit, listen, obey, and execute. Essentially, this teacher-directed-style took the hard work out of learning, embracing the following mindset:

Let me show you how to do this.
Let me tell you what you are doing wrong.
Let me tell you what I think.
Let me tell you what to do.

This suited me fine because I did not have to think too hard. Stephen would have none of this, for passive learning was not enough. Expressive performance requires active participation and teachers like Stephen force students to question and to think for themselves. As I became more engaged in my own learning my motivation levels skyrocketed. This episode profoundly affected my musical progress and, more generally, my learning progress. It was probably the most valuable learning experience I experienced as a young adult, and I always will be thankful to Stephen for that.

Questioning

The simplest strategy for increasing student metacognition is to ask more questions. [26] Simple open-ended questions prompt self-discovery. Here are some examples.

- How do you think you played?

---

26 Teachers, however, should not ask questions while students are playing. This does not prevent errors or encourage self-learning.

- Tell me what you hear. How does it sound to you?
- Is what you're doing working? Why? Why not?
- Which goals would you like to set for this week?
- What can you do to learn this passage thoroughly?
- Can you explain what you are doing? What are you thinking?
- What have you improved upon since last week?
- Can you teach me how to do this?

When students respond to questions teachers must wait patiently and allow them to struggle to find the right words. They should try to resist the temptation to put words into the mouths of students and remember that struggle is necessary for learning. Teaching and giving answers are not synonymous. Nor is learning and having the answers supplied. Aldous Huxley was acutely aware of this when he wrote his essay *The Dangers of Good Teaching* in 1927:

> Working on the old-fashioned system, the clever teacher (deplorable paradox!) does almost more harm than the stupid one. For the clever schoolmaster makes things too easy for his pupils; he relieves them of the necessity of finding out things for themselves. By dint of brilliant teaching he succeeds in almost eliminating the learning process. He knows how to fill his pupils with ready-made knowledge, which they inevitably forget (since it is not their knowledge and cost them nothing to acquire), as soon as the examination for which it was required is safely passed.
>
> The stupid teacher, on the other hand, may be so completely intolerable that the child will perhaps be driven, despairingly and in mere self-defence, to educate himself; in which case the incompetent shepherd will have done, all unwittingly, a great service to his charge, by forcing him into a rebellious intellectual independence.

Initially musical understanding is *procedural*. That is, students know how to do things but cannot necessarily explain the process. Declarative knowledge is the ability to talk and think about music using linguistic terms. Allowing students to talk about concepts in their own words strengthens musical understanding from the procedural realm to include the declarative realm. Words are terribly important for they enable us to think. We cannot think complex thoughts without them. To deepen conceptual understanding we need the power of words, and we must be able to articulate with them.

Verbal Mediation

Abraham Lincoln's secretary asked him, "Sir, why do you read aloud to yourself, and why do you talk to yourself?" Lincoln's response was, "When I do this, I remember twice as much, for twice as long." [27] This is verbal mediation, another strategy for increasing metacognition.

Verbal mediation attempts to describe our thinking. When we describe what we are doing, either to ourselves or to someone else, we learn well. I use this technique when students encounter a learning difficulty. "Tell me what you are thinking," I ask them. By thinking out loud as they practise students often uncover the root of a problem and gain a better understanding of the task. Teachers, on the other hand, get insight into students' mental processes. More generally, reading aloud helps us process information in the mind and stay in the present. This is why discussion and debate are so important; they clarify the mind.

Most children have one music lesson a week and receive little guidance in between. Hence, learning how to learn is essential, and solo music practice provides an opportunity for this. The process of learning music encourages metacognitive skills. Professional musicians demonstrate a high degree of metacognition in terms of performance preparation, concentration, monitoring quality, and performance evaluation. Professional musicians have a high degree of awareness of their strengths and weaknesses. Stephen Covey writes that self-awareness is "our capacity to stand apart from ourselves and examine our thinking, our motives, our history, our scripts, our actions and our habits and tendencies" (48).

---

27 See Stephen Chandler's book *100 Ways to Motivate Yourself.*

Metacognition provides us with this objective view of our strengths and weaknesses. Through reflection and evaluation, we understand our actions more critically. We keep improving our learning by designing and redesigning our training. We question the status quo, and our actions determine our progress. Albert Einstein attributed his success to curiosity, determination, and hard work. "Never stop questioning," he said. Great learners ask great questions.

Reflection

Learning without thought is labour lost. Thought without learning is perilous. - Confucius

Metacognition starts with reflection.

In *The Apology*, Socrates writes, "The unreflected life is not worth living." However, Confucius says activity and reflection must complement and support each other. Action by itself is blind, but reflection alone is impotent.

Making time for reflection before and after a learning activity is important. Teenage boys lag behind girls in reflective skills. They tend to overestimate their capabilities and underestimate the time it takes for learning to occur. Creating opportunities for reflection is simple. In my course Music and Keyboard in the Classroom, students make comments on a 'reflection page.' This might be goal setting at the beginning of the lesson and/or evaluation at the end. Verbally I model appropriate statements in regard to goal setting, task difficulties, improvement strategies, strengths and weaknesses, and self-evaluation.

- What are the requirements of this task?
- What can I achieve in this practice session?
- What am I finding difficult?
- Which strategies do I use to fix the problem?
- Can I play the piece well?

Below are some reflective comments from a grade-seven class I taught in 2009.

"I just mastered lesson seven. I'm so pleased because it's been really difficult for me."

"There's one section in lesson eight I just cannot get. I think I need to repeat it a lot."

"Jessie just helped me with lesson five. It makes more sense now."

"Keyboard is becoming easier and more fun. Today I completed two pieces, which is amazing!"

"I definitely improved my technique, which I think is great."

"Some things are a bit challenging, but with time I could get used to playing the keyboard."

"I am surprised and happy because Sir thinks I have a good sense of rhythm."

"I'm getting better and better every day! I should be proud of myself, and I am!"

As a teacher, I get excited reading these comments. I also get insight into how students are thinking about their learning, and I can monitor their metacognitive progress. This reflective process helps students to become intrinsically motivated and independent learners.

> *Man's release from tutelage is enlightenment. His tutelage is his inability to make use of his understanding without guidance from another. - Immanuel Kant*

In summary, I have discussed three strategies for developing metacognition in students: questioning, verbal mediation, and explicit reflection.

Probably the best way to gain insights into the learning process is to teach someone else, which I explore earlier in this chapter. Teaching is a dynamic mix of reflection, questioning, and explaining with continual feedback from the learner. It wins the gold medal in the metacognition event.

Chapter Four

Playing Music with the Whole Brain

With Instrument With Notation	Without Instrument With Notation
With Instrument Without Notation	Without Instrument Without Notation

Figure 21: The Four Learning Modes

There are various ways of practising and performing music, and these are processed in different parts of the brain. Reading music is predominantly a left-hemisphere action. Playing by ear, improvising, playing from memory, and playing in one's imagination activate more of the right hemisphere. For a well-rounded and more robust musicianship, teachers and learners should consider a balanced whole-brain practice structure.

Essentially, early childhood music education chooses between an emphasis on learning notation and associated theory, or an aural listen-copy approach. My preference is for the latter. Just as we learn to speak before we read and understand grammatical rules, so we should learn music through a 'sound before notation' framework. Suzuki called this the 'mother tongue approach' because of the parallels to learning language. Some teachers worry when young children play music without notation. My first piano teacher was quite concerned about my inclination for playing by ear, and she asked my mother to discourage me from doing this at home. [28] This teacher's well-intentioned concern was that I would have difficulty achieving a level of reading fluency if my preferred medium was playing by ear. As music becomes more difficult, however, notation becomes necessary for progress, and so an appropriate time for its introduction presents itself. If we parallel learning to read notation with language, most children start formal reading around the age of six. One way to introduce notation is to start with the notation of music a child already can perform. Then a teacher should move to pieces the child has not learned to play but knows and finally begin with the notation of unfamiliar repertoire.

Children who learn by ear do not necessarily become poor sight-readers, but they are advantaged in learning to hear and understand music internally. Playing by ear and improvising are fundamental ingredients for developing overall musicianship during the early stages of a child's musical development. Furthermore an ability to engage in aural learning modes can be attributed to other positive and long-lasting effects. A 1999 study by K.A. Glenn found "students who were taught by ear in the initial stages were more likely to continue learning their instrument

---

28   Fortunately for me my mother did not take this advice.

and were reported by their teacher to be more motivated and to enjoy their playing more than the other group" (49).

With Instrument, With Notation

Reading Music

Fail not to practise the reading of old clefs; otherwise many treasures of past times will remain a closed fountain to you. - Robert Schumann

In the West, reading musical notation is probably the most common method of learning and performing music. Nevertheless some musicians are more adept at playing without musical notation than with it, and many successful musicians from the worlds of jazz, pop, and folk cannot read music. What incentive is there for students to spend the time and effort required in order to become literate with music notation?

Formal musical knowledge may not be an essential part of musicianship, but it certainly enriches it. If you need motivation, or are looking to motivate others to learn how to read music, consider the following.

1. Most ensembles and choirs require communication with other musicians through notation. Even jazz ensembles, and particularly big bands, rely heavily on written notation.
2. Notation is the basis of music theory, which provides a pathway to a depth of musical understanding not possible without it. Theory helps us to understand the conceptual and to talk declaratively about music. It can open up a new world of musical understanding and illuminate the 'why' as well as the 'what' and the 'how.'
3. The ability to read music enables exploration of libraries full of new music otherwise not available to us.
4. Much music, particularly Western art music, is too difficult to learn by ear. If we want to play the extraordinary but complex repertoires of the great composers, reading is the only means.

5. Learning from notation demands a precision and a series of checkpoints that will improve aspects of musicianship.

Beware of the attitude that spurns reading music. Not being able to read music can stifle musical development. I have yet to meet a non-reader who does not regret his or her decision not to invest the time required to learn to read music.

Sight-Reading

Poor sight-reading has been identified as one of the reasons students stop lessons (50). The most effective way to become a successful sight-reader is to practise the skill regularly. Just as with reading a book, in time students will recognise clusters of notes as phrases rather than as individual entities. There is a correlation between proficient sight-reading and time spent practising it. You do not become fluent at reading anything without regular practice. Everyone who can read a book has the intellectual capacity to become an effective sight-reader, but improving sight-reading requires a continual increase in the difficulty of the material. The beauty of this skill is that it speeds up the learning process and opens up new and wider opportunities for making music with others. Learning to sight-read involves a different mindset than when one learns for a performance. Maintaining fluency and momentum is paramount. In particular one must not stop to correct mistakes, for in sight-reading mistakes are tolerated. Practising with a metronome, backing tracks, or better still, live ensemble partners, can help to induce this required musical continuity.

When I was learning piano, my sight-reading was comparatively weak. The teacher's advice was to obtain a stack of suitably difficult music and practise sight-reading every day. My teacher told me that once I had played a piece the sight-playing experience was over, which is why I needed the ready supply of new music. Teachers should include sight-reading in their lessons because students are unlikely to practise this skill at home if they don't see it to be valued during lessons.

Successful sight-readers keep their eyes on the music more often than poorer sight-readers. This is one of the reasons many pianists struggle with sight-reading, as it is difficult to keep the eyes on the music while making hand movements to the correct keys. Eighteenth-century German musician and composer Carl Philipp Emanuel Bach once advised, "If you want to improve your sight-reading, practise in the dark." This can be simulated by closing the eyes during practice. Improving the sense of touch allows the eyes to spend more time on the music on the page, which in turn facilitates better sight-reading.

Sight-reading is a multitasking skill that involves playing the current measure while scanning the next, moving fingers to the keys without looking, using prior musical knowledge to comprehend the music, and relating to the music on an emotional level. Better sight-readers have a greater knowledge of musical styles and repertoire, which provides a database of familiarity for the chunking process. This familiarity enables sight-readers to make educated guesses when necessary to maintain the flow of the music. Effective sight-readers scan the music before a performance, while considering the tempo, the time and key signatures, and possible difficulties. Rhythmic reading is the most important and challenging musical component of sight-reading. One can practise this in isolation, even away from one's instrument. Rhythmic reading exercises can readily be sourced. For those wishing to improve this aspect of their musicianship, I recommend the approach below. The fundamental of this approach is to relate rhythm to pulse. To be rhythmically strong requires an awareness of the beats of the pulse.

Here is the rhythm to an excerpt of Brahms's *Academic Festival Overture*.

Figure 22: Rhythmic Reading

Teachers should ask students to do the following:

1. Isolate and write out the rhythm for practice, as shown above.
2. Add the pulse counts, as shown above. (Over time this will be less necessary, but for now do not assume the student can do this.)
3. Ensure the student understands the distribution of accents. 'S' means a strong accent; 'W' means weak.

Figure 23: Rhythmic Stress Distribution

4. Clap the rhythm while counting the pulse out loud.
5. Clap the pulse and sing the rhythm to 'da.'
6. On a table, tap the left hand to the pulse and the right hand to the rhythm.
7. On a table, tap the right hand to the pulse and the left hand to the rhythm.

With Instrument, Without Notation

Playing from Memory

For musicians, an ability to play from memory opens up the world of practising via the imagination, which grants freedom from notation. Performing from memory indicates a deep understanding and internalization of the music.

Playing from memory involves performing a piece one has learned as a result of rehearsing with notation, to the point where notation is no longer required as a guide. Some musicians claim that memorization allows them to develop their expressive ideas more freely and to communicate those ideas more effectively. One study found that an audience with musical training rated memorised performances higher in terms of communicative ability (51). An audience feels a greater connection when notation and music stands are omitted, and when distractions such as page turning are not an issue.

Playing from memory is a skill that should be encouraged during lesson time. Young musicians can start by memorizing easy pieces they like, as they already will have a mental idea of what the piece sounds like. Remember that early success in any endeavour is important for confidence, so musicians should consider the constraints of short-term memory. Rather than aiming to play an entire piece from memory too soon, focus on a given section, perhaps no more than a phrase or a couple of measures at a time. Even a small weekly target will develop this skill, and the process of trying to play from memory is in itself a valuable exercise.

Studies of chess players, athletes, mathematicians, and musicians suggest that a good memory tends to be domain specific. Increasingly complex memory loads form due to specific subject knowledge of how to chunk and categorise data. Everyone is capable of improving memory skills in his or her area of interest. Learning to play music from memory requires an understanding of musical-chunking processes, which is greatly assisted by understanding the score. Teachers play a role in developing this knowledge by asking exploratory and analytical questions. Here are some examples.

- Describe the piece to me. What is the form?
- Tell me about the major themes and how they are treated in terms of modulations, sequences, and so on. How are these themes linked? Play through the piece slowly, commentating on these features.
- Where are the climaxes in the music?
- Discuss prevalent harmonic structures. Where does the composer use tonic-dominant harmonies on this page?
- Which melodies and rhythms do you find the most difficult to play? Please sing them for me.
- What are your favourite sections in the piece?

Verbal mediation enhances musical 'big picture' thinking and provides a structure for learning from memory. Some people visualise the musical score as they play. Others sing the main melody in their head, imagining the contours of the music. Rehearsing the piece mentally, away from the instrument, and hearing the music in the mind are important for memory work. I use air flights as opportunities to practise my musical memory. I close my eyes and imagine playing the piano keys as I sing the piece in my mind. I do this slowly, and if I cannot visualise a note, I know my learning is not yet secure. Sometimes I take this a step further, moving my fingers on the tray table. My phone has PDF files of my repertoire so I can further analyse the structure of the music. This in turn generates more chunking possibilities. Learning from memory requires a greater time commitment than using the score as well as further time in the maintenance of memorised repertoire. Over time the ear learns to take a larger responsibility for the lack of notation, and the process becomes easier.

For many musicians, memorised performance creates performance anxiety. These become less stressful as musicians experience performance success and learn to trust in the learning process. Stress is the enemy of memory. Consequently, worrying about a memory lapse may well be the cause of it. Learning to play from memory is primarily a right-brain skill, but when musicians worry about memory retrieval the focus shifts to the left hemisphere, and the memory-rescue problem persists. Practising in nervous situations will improve resilience to stress. Sometimes I learn the most difficult parts of a new piece first and challenge myself to convert these passages into easy bits. Unlike beginner musicians I rarely start practising from the beginning of a piece but proceed from many different starting points. If I do suffer a memory lapse, I will be in better shape to recover quickly.

Some people can play a piece from memory but like to have their music on the stand as a backup. This has never worked for me. I find that it confuses my brain, so for me it has to be one way or the other. I recall an occasion when I was playing piano in an outdoor concert with the school band. As we performed, a gust of wind blew away my music, and I panicked and lost my place. What surprised me was that I actually knew my part well and had no need for sheet music. Yet when I had the music in front of me it seemed like another part of my brain was taking over and being relied upon. If only I had a button to press so I could toggle my cognitive processes between the two hemispheres.

Practising in different physical environments is an effective way to strengthen memory. As we learn, our senses are receptive to the immediate environment, and the information we want to store becomes associated and connected with this environment. Specifically, the more ways in which musical information can be encoded the more likely one is to remember the material. If your instrument is portable, consider practising in different spaces, such as the bedroom, the lounge room, the garage, or even outdoors. Pianists should find unfamiliar pianos to play, as this prepares them for real-life situations. Beginner musicians require a private and quiet environment so they can concentrate and get into the flow of their learning. Children are susceptible to interruptions to concentration, and in this age of instant communication they require encouragement regarding the self-discipline required to regulate these diversions. Advanced musicians occasionally choose to practise in a difficult environment, such as a noisy one, to test their mettle.

Like most choral conductors I have my choirs perform repertoire from memory. In my early career, though, I assumed choirs had memorization limits. One day a colleague challenged me by saying, "Michael, they know a lot more than you think they do." Since then I have pressed my choirs to memorise all repertoire, and we practise this at every rehearsal. In 2005 I took a girls' choir from Australia to Europe. Three weeks before departure we decided to learn and memorise Benjamin Britten's twenty-minute song cycle 'A Ceremony of Carols'. The girls not only achieved this, but did so during the stressful period of final exams. Children are so capable. Teachers, coaches, mentors, and conductors should not let their preconceptions limit their students' potential. Children will work to the standard demanded by the teacher. As a footnote to the European tour story above, we were performing 'A Ceremony of Carols' at the acoustically superb and gothic Minorite

Monastery in Wels, Austria, and I had left the score in my hotel room. The girls were greatly amused that I would have to put my memory to the test. I had not practised conducting this piece without the score, and I was in front of a discerning and capacity audience. I berated myself; this was the first time I had forgotten to bring my score to a performance. Following the concert the girls unanimously proclaimed this performance as being our best in Europe. Perhaps this was because of the heightened communication the choir and I shared. With no score to focus on my eyes remained in contact with the choir. I missed a couple of cues, but on the whole my memory survived. This was a *flow* experience; the challenge required my fullest mental ability. [29]

Playing by Ear

Playing by ear is less frequently encouraged in traditional music lessons, which is surprising, given that most musicians would love to develop this skill. Why is the ability to play without music considered second rate to sight-reading? For many students the lack of this ability creates deep reservations about their musical skills. Furthermore students who can play in aural-based and creative ways—such as playing by ear, playing without music, and improvising—are more likely to continue to participate in musical activity in post-school life (52). Educators in Finland are acting on this research. Music schools now require classical piano instruction to include non-classical elements such as 'comping' (a chord-based accompaniment style) and improvisation. This is based on the idea that classical music skills and understandings are not necessarily transferable to other types of music. The government provides training and assistance to help teachers adapt to these new techniques.

Some teachers equate playing by ear with fixed genetic ability and believe it cannot be taught; however, it can be learned. Through sustained practice everyone can improve his or her aural acuity and learn to play by ear. Also, teachers might not encourage playing by ear

---

29 There is no recording of this particular performance, but you can listen to another performance by the same choir at St. Nicholas in Prague at www.musiceducationworld.com.

because of how they were taught. There is an old saying: "Teachers teach how they themselves were taught". Avoiding this requires vigilance to prevent perpetuating dated practices of the past.

If you always do what you've always done, you'll always get what you've always got. - anonymous

Being able to play by ear can create spontaneous and satisfying opportunities for making music. In 1991 I was performing for a business event for the premier of South Australia. I was playing a classical repertoire, and the event organiser hurried toward me with a special request. It was the night of Princess Diana's funeral, and our premier wanted me to play 'Goodbye England's Rose' during a two-minute silence. Although I was put on the spot, my ability to play by ear enabled me to get the job done. In fact when I used to play this style of music more regularly most of the repertoire I played was by ear. Along with developing my musicianship skills it was a great way to save money on sheet music.

When I was a young boy my home environment fostered my ability to play by ear. My mother whistled tunes and asked me to copy them. My uncle encouraged creative musical learning by teaching me to play common pieces many music teachers dread, such as 'Chopsticks' and 'Heart and Soul.' Family encouragement and support are important for young musicians. Students are more successful in all aspects of learning when respected role models show interest in their success. My family support and the interest they displayed helped generate my avid musical curiosity. In my life there were two sides to music, and both were equally satisfying. I liked the serious repertoire of classical examination music and I enjoyed tinkering with non-notated pieces aurally and creatively.

To develop the ear computer-based aural training programs abound, but I think the trial-and-error method of playing music is the best way to learn. The idea is to start with simple melodies and gradually increase the level of difficulty to eventually incorporate harmony. [30] Ear training

---

30 This assumes that your instrument is a harmonic one.

takes time, but teachers can help support development. In the following exercise students must fill in the missing notes. This concept works well because children love the challenge of problem solving. Any game that involves incomplete information is a sure way to drive curiosity. Beethoven's 'Ode to Joy' is simple, but teachers can devise similar exercises at suitable levels for their students.

Figure 24: Excerpt from *What Tune is This?*
Fun, Practical Aural for Young Musicians
By Michael Griffin

Jazz pianist Oscar Peterson had an astonishing ability to reproduce sounds in his head. As he put it, all musical ideas originate in the brain. To develop his remarkable facility he sang a melodic phrase then attempted to copy it on the piano. He then extended the challenge by playing two hands one octave, then two octaves, apart. This is an excellent way to train the ear and develop hand-ear coordination. Louis Armstrong, Errol Garner, Chet Baker, Paul McCartney, and Bono could not read music, but they could all play by ear. During my work as a pianist on Hayman Island, I met Dick Rudolph, who wrote the number-one hit 'Loving You' for his wife, Minnie Ripperton, in 1975. Dick and I spent some time together playing piano and sharing ideas. Dick told me that what we were doing was similar to how he went about writing songs. His method was informal. Notation was not part of his creative process, but he loved *playing* with musical ideas and was able to vary and extend his simple ideas in a musically satisfying way.

New ideas come to people through play and experimentation. How much time and encouragement do we give students to play with their musical ideas? Play allows for an adventure into the unknown.

> *Play is the serious business of childhood.*
> *- Jean Piaget (1896–1980), Swiss biologist and psychologist.*

Without Instrument, With Notation

I suppose I was not practising the piano enough in my university years because my piano teacher suggested I practise in transit from my home to university, on the train. This, Stephen said, would be a constructive way to use my time. Following his advice I placed the sheet music on my lap, swallowed my pride, and using my imagination, started to play. What a revelation! I did not need my instrument to rehearse music. The brain constructs learning through mental imagery and imagination.

> Q. Why should children bother to attend band rehearsal if they forget to bring their instrument?
> A. Because they can still learn through mental imagery.

I take this a step further. When a young musician once declared, "Sir, I cannot come to rehearsal because I forgot my trombone," I put his mind at ease. "These things happen," I said, "but rest easy because you can still attend rehearsal." Providing him with spare sheet music, I had the boy make realistic movements with embouchure and arms, as if he were playing 'air' trombone. To make this look as real as possible required the use of his musical imagination. The boy thought I was a little crazy for asking him to do this but here was an opportunity to teach the band a new learning concept. [31] Likewise with the choir, although I would not ask a student with a sore throat to sing they would still be required to attend rehearsal and mouth the words *without instrument, with notation*.

---

31 Interestingly the boy did not forget his trombone again.

Score reading engages the musical imagination without the extra demand of physical performance. This cognitive rehearsal enables students to imagine the muscle movements that would be engaged in performance and provides insights into the musical structure and intricacies of a work that are difficult to obtain from merely listening. This visual clarity can enhance the pleasure of a listening experience. In addition, mobile devices can store digital sheet music, which can provide unlimited opportunities for private study.

Without Instrument, Without Notation

In recent years brain-scanning techniques have revealed the true ability of the brain to learn via the imagination. In one experiment the brain of a young violinist was scanned to compare two conditions: 1) playing the violin with notation; and 2) imagining the playing of that same music with no violin and no notation. The scans revealed almost exactly the same neural firing and circuitry formation. Norman Doidge describes a similar 'imagination' experiment in which two groups of subjects who had not learned piano were taught a simple sequence of notes. Both groups sat at pianos, but only one group physically played. The other group imagined playing the piano. Brain mapping occurred before, during, and after the experiment. Remarkably, imagined (mental) practice produced similar physical changes in the brain to actual physical practice (27). Doidge states, "We can change our brain anatomy simply by using our imagination. Thoughts, repeated in mental practice, strengthen the existing neuronal connections and make new ones."

I recall a story about a professional golfer who, after being released from a year in prison, played an excellent round of golf. When his golfing buddies asked how this was possible given that he had no opportunity to practise, he replied, "But I did practise. I played eighteen holes every day up here, in my imagination." Mentally, this man had attended to all the details as he usually would in a typical round of golf. His imaginary game took about the same time to play as a real game of golf.

Once I had the fortune to attend a workshop with legendary jazz trumpeter Bobby Shew. He used to play with John Coltrane, and in the workshop he recollected some interesting and amusing personal anecdotes. Shew told us that Coltrane often practised without his saxophone. When flying to a gig most of the musicians would have a few drinks, but not Coltrane. He closed his eyes and mentally practised on a piece of wood. Shew calls this type of practice 'ideo-kinetics.'

These examples support that the brain does become active through mental imagery. Thinking about an action causes the same electrical discharge in the brain as the action itself. Therefore, mental practice is an effective way to practise music when physical practice is not possible, and for its own sake. Perhaps a contributing factor to Mozart's genius was that his thoughts were always on music. "You know that I am, so to speak, swallowed up in music," he told his father, "that I am busy with it all day—speculating, studying, considering."

Many of Mozart's works that, according to history, seem to have been composed on the spur of the moment, were most likely swimming around in his conscious and unconscious minds, fermenting for long periods of time.

Music is enough for a lifetime, but a lifetime is not enough for music.
- Sergei Rachmaninoff

The combinations for practising and playing music with and without music notation and/or an instrument offer challenges for a lifetime.

- Reading and understanding notation to reproduce a pre-existing piece of music authentically.
- Sight-reading.
- Playing from memory pieces that have been learned with notation.
- Playing by ear.
- Improvising.

Few musicians will be able to devote the time required to become proficient in all of these modes of playing music, but it is a worthy goal to pursue, and one that will improve all-around musicianship and more fully engage the entire brain.

Whole-brain education recognises the inseparability of cognition and emotion and involves the right and left hemispheres, cerebral cortex, and limbic system. Whole-brain learning has been a key ingredient in the annals of human genius. Albert Einstein is a classic example of someone who harnessed the power of the whole brain. Einstein believed in the power of the imagination to generate ideas and solve problems. He inspired his imagination by playing music and daydreaming. [32] "If I were not a physicist," he said, "I would probably be a musician. I often think in music. I live my daydreams in music. I see my life in terms of music."

Einstein's wife, Elsa, revealed that music was not simply a diversion but an essential factor that inspired his scientific work. Strange as it might seem, spawning ideas in one discipline sometimes requires a focus on another. "Music helps him when he is thinking about his theories," she said. "He goes to his study, comes back, strikes a few chords on the piano, and jots something down, then returns to his study."

Real musical experience makes comprehensive use of the brain's ability to think and feel simultaneously. Neuroscientist Frank Wilson stated, "Active 'musicing' is possibly more whole-brain than any known activity." [33] Making music involves brain functions in both hemispheres simultaneously. It even occupies more areas of our brain than language.

---

32 Einstein started piano lessons at age six, but he began to make real progress at the age of thirteen when he discovered Mozart's sonatas (2).
33 From a lecture at the California Music Education Association Convention, 1989.

CHAPTER FIVE

MUSICAL CREATIVITY

There is nothing more marvellous than thinking of a new idea.
There is nothing more magnificent than seeing a new idea working.
There is nothing more useful than a new idea that serves your purpose.
- Edward de Bono (53)

A general perception is that making music is inherently creative, but this is not so. Many who learn an instrument seldom engage in the cores of creative music—composing, improvising, and rearranging. Rather, music education programs focus mostly on the re-creation of pre-existing music to the extent that little time is set aside for creative exploration and expression. Being creative with music is best achieved by *playing* with music but not necessarily in the company of the teacher. The process of becoming musically creative is open to all. Anyone can attempt to alter notes in a melody, re-harmonise a melody, play without music, copy a melody, or improvise.

In broader terms, free imaginative play is crucial for social, emotional, and cognitive development. 'Free play' refers to unstructured play in that the activity need not have an obvious function or a clear goal. Games might be fun ways to learn socially, emotionally, and cognitively, but free play is different. Unlike games, that have an existing set of rules that have grown or that someone else created, free play has no rules and thereby generates more creative possibilities and responses. This challenges the brain more than following predetermined rules because children are required to use their imagination and try new ideas. Recent evidence suggests that a lack of opportunity for unstructured and imaginative free play in childhood can affect children's later social development, behavioural flexibility, ability to cope with stress, and development of problem-solving skills. Since the early 1980s, a trend has arisen in which children's free playtime is diminishing. Parents may underestimate the value of free play in favour of more structured activities that are assumed to deliver more valuable learning outcomes.

Students who learn in creative ways learn well. Creative learning is fun, engaging, and motivating. It requires identifying problems, considering multiple possibilities, making decisions, and finding solutions. Creative people are more likely to have adopted a growth-intelligence-mindset. They are prepared to take risks and are prepared to fail. They understand the value and necessity of making mistakes. Creative people are open to new experiences. They allow their imaginations to be inspired by anything and everything, including the sounds around them, nature, art, and music. They have heroes and role models, and delight in examples of excellence. While an individual cannot be creative without acting intelligently, creative people are not necessarily the smartest in their domain. In the confines of the old IQ system there is a correlation linking creativity with intelligence only up to the threshold score of approximately 120. This implies that creative people need to be fairly intelligent but not excessively so.

At the pinnacle of musical creativity is the ability to compose and improvise. Jazz improvisation requires serious engagement underpinned by a consummate level of musicianship. Simultaneously the improviser's short-term memory must attend to harmony, melodies and patterns, form, musical expression, and rhythm to produce meaningful and contextual melodies on the fly. [34] For pianists the challenge is even greater as they are also required to accompany themselves with the left hand while the right hand improvises. This requires voicing rootless chords with a bass player and constructing a bass line

---

34 Not surprisingly, creativity experts have a found a correlation between creative people and the capacity of their short-term memories.

when playing as a soloist. An essential requirement for improvisation is the ability to take risks and a preparedness to make mistakes. In improvisation, a mistake is not a mistake until the next note puts the former note into context. As Dave Brubeck said "There is no such thing as a wrong note – so long as it can be resolved". Thus, if a musician plays a wrong note or makes a poor note choice, they can correct it with the next note. Such 'wrong' notes can even provide new impetus and inspiration for the rest of the improvisation. In this way mistakes ultimately can become catalysts for creativity.

The abilities to play by ear and from memory increase the potential to improvise. Competent improvising, however, requires both structure and freedom. Without structure, there is chaos; with too much structure there's no creativity. Gaining proficiency with jazz structures involves a great deal of rote learning. Melodic patterns, chord progressions, chord voicing, and harmonies must be rendered to a level of automation to free up short-term memory for stylistic considerations. To master this ability, jazz improvisers practise their repertoires and associated patterns in several keys, and sometimes in all twelve. As improvisers become fully engaged with their craft they become totally absorbed and find *flow*. 'Freedom' also refers to freedom from self-consciousness and inhibition. Scientists have found that a region of the brain linked to inhibition is less active in jazz musicians than in other musicians who do not improvise (54).

Ten Suggestions for Fostering Musical Creativity

1. The most limited resource in education is time. Playing with ideas takes time. Allocate sufficient time to experiment with musical ideas. Jean-Jacques Rousseau said, "The most useful rule of education is: Do not save time but lose it" (55). Creative learning requires personal space. Music programmes need a lot of time for children to grow and develop with musical ideas.
2. Maximize opportunities to give choice. Teachers should allow students the freedom to approach an activity *their* way.

This increases intrinsic motivation and gives students a sense of ownership. Learning can happen spontaneously through self-discovery and does not always require the presence of a teacher. Teachers should provide opportunities for self-initiated learning and avoid overly detailed supervision. Over-teaching can be harmful. Teachers should also allow students to engage in discovery learning of their choice, fuelled by *their* curiosity and excitement. Children should experience the joy of learning by doing, playing, exploring, discovering, and sharing. One cannot force learning upon someone; learning is a personal activity in which knowledge is acquired. Students must have opportunities to construct conceptual understandings by themselves.

3. Authentic problem finding is an important concept for composition. Teachers should find authentic problems to solve that are relevant to their students. One example of this is the protest song. As Rousseau says, adolescence is the age when children are ready for the education of values, ethics, and morals. Such a time of ethical flowering offers wonderful opportunities for student creativity.

    The story of Dave Carroll exemplifies authentic problem finding. In 2009 Carroll's guitar was damaged on a flight. Following nine months of ineffective complaint letters and phone calls, he warned the airline that his next approach would be to post a protest song on YouTube. Carroll subsequently uploaded two music videos about his experience with the airline. Both videos received several million views. The significant publicity resulted in the airline offering him compensation for the damaged guitar. After exhausting the traditional channels of customer complaints Carroll recognised a powerful and creative medium to make a statement. YouTube, at the time a relatively new social media platform, effectively had rebalanced the relationship between consumer and company. Protest songs are not new. They were popular in the 1960s with jazz artists such as Nina Simone, The Beatles, and Bob Dylan. Protest songs continue to be an essential aspect of popular music culture, which is one of the prime reasons teenagers gravitate toward this kind of music. Meaningful goals offer fertile ground for creative learning, but creative output needs an audience. Audiences give feedback and provide a sense of purpose.

4. Creativity demands questioning. Teachers should encourage *a lot* of questions and tease out questions for students to solve. Teachers can be in too much of a hurry to satisfy their students' curiosity; they should allow their students to find answers rather than providing answers for them.

> *Let him sit with the problem for a while and solve it himself.*
> *Let him know nothing because you have told him, but because*
> *he has learnt it for himself. Let the children discover.*
> *- Jean-Jacques Rousseau (55)*

Allowing questions to remain unanswered for a time will arouse intense curiosity. This can be exploited and even contrived by presenting incomplete or contradictory information about a topic. It is this lack of completeness that compels one to understand it further.

> *Wonder is the seed of knowledge. - Francis Bacon*

5. Think, work, and play divergently. Teachers should allow students to challenge key assumptions and break rules. In schools, much of education is convergent in that student work heads toward a singular pre-existing answer. Teachers should not fall into the science trap. Students rarely conduct experiments in science classes; they undertake contrived demonstrations designed to converge with an expected and known outcome. Creativity is about exploring possibilities and choosing from a range of solutions. Divergence in music-making is evident through musical interpretation and improvisation. For example, how can a simple musical idea be varied and extended?

   Teachers should engage students with the concept of 'idea improvement.' Edward de Bono says, "Most people look for creative solutions when things are not going well, but continuous improvement even when things are going well is an area ripe for creative thinking" (53). Complacency and self-satisfaction spurn creative improvement.

Teachers also should use the word 'imagine' in their teaching. Imagination is the capacity to think in terms of possibility, an essential ingredient for creative outcomes. Children will see many possibilities that teachers may not.

Never stop imagining. Imagination is greater than knowledge.
- Albert Einstein

6. Teachers should inspire students through personal, historical, and peer examples. Heroes open our eyes, show us what is possible, and redefine the boundaries of possibility. Teachers ought to take students to concerts performed by professional musicians and by students of the same age. Students need opportunities to collaborate on musical projects with others. Real learning occurs when likeminded people share ideas. Historical examples of greatness can remove the mythology of prodigious achievement. Students should receive the message that substantial preparatory work always precedes a master-piece. For example, Beethoven's *Ninth Symphony* required at least ten years of study and was inspired by other works. These included Beethoven's own *Choral Fantasia* and Mozart's lesser-known *Misericordias Domini in D Minor, K 222*. Beethoven recorded much of his compositional planning, idea development, and constant revision in his prodigious collection of sketchbooks.
7. Teachers should draw connections between music and nature, music and numbers, music and sports, and music and art by using metaphors and analogies. All things in the universe are related and new patterns and understandings continually emerge. Creative people find relationships the rest of us never notice. For many students, the pattern-rich disciplines of math-ematics and music offer many opportunities for connectedness.
8. For creative tasks, formative feedback is more important than evaluation. Grades and quantitative measures, labelling, and

tracking undermine intrinsic motivation and are sure ways to shut down creative effort. Instead of offering extrinsic rewards teachers should encourage children to appreciate and be pleased with their own creative efforts. Instead of comparing their creative work with others students should reflect verbally on their work. Teachers must be mindful of their own preoccupation with judgement and comparison.

9. To encourage risk-taking in a nonthreatening atmosphere, teachers should provide conditions for relaxed and enjoyable learning. Worrying about mistakes stifles creative effort because innovation requires experimentation, which implies uncertain outcomes and being prepared for mistakes. Creative people fail more often than non-creative people because they see mistakes as necessary for learning. This preparedness to take risks is a sign of a growth-intelligence mindset.

Success is going from failure to failure without losing enthusiasm. - Winston Churchill

Creativity is allowing yourself to make mistakes. Art is knowing which ones to keep.
- Scott Adams, American cartoonist, b.1957

10. Creativity does not mean 'anything goes.' 'Bizarre' is not necessarily creative. Creativity is more about an appropriate but unexpected response. It requires discipline and making deliberate and informed choices. Creative people are highly metacognitive. They know *why* they do *what* they do. Creativity does not need to be complex, but it does need to have purpose.

A theory is the more impressive the greater is the simplicity of its premises, the more different are the kinds of things it relates and the more extended the range of its applicability. - Albert Einstein

Working in Groups

Formal music lessons seldom include free creative activities, so young people form groups and design their own. They learn musical skills by watching and imitating their peers in jam sessions that centre on play and enjoyment. This learning is intrinsically motivated and highly meta-cognitive and involves higher-order learning skills. Participants think out aloud, bounce ideas off one another, teach and encourage one another, and make decisions. Students often can explain concepts to their peers better than adult teachers can because they share a more similar vocabulary and mindset. In *Fantasia of the Unconscious*, D.H. Lawrence writes, "Adults always interfere—they don't understand childish intelligence." Children often learn in ways that adults do not teach. Lucy Green offers the following sensible advice: "By understanding how children construct a method for teaching themselves, music teachers may discover alternative methods for creating a learning environment" (56).

If teachers are involved in group settings they will need to adjust to their new role. To begin with it would be wise for them to spend time observing the group dynamics and learning behaviours of their students. It is the students who now take greater responsibility for their learning and for the learning of their peers. The rewards of group learning are significant. Students learn about shared expertise and responsibility and how to teach one another. They become increasingly autonomous, hence more interested in their learning.

Music activities provide an authentic opportunity for group work, for ensemble work will not be productive without respect for one another's skills. Under the guidance of an astute teacher, students learn to listen to one another with a sense of tolerance, politeness, and respect, and make contributions in a safe and nonthreatening environment. They develop leadership skills as well as the ability to form empathic relationships. Musicians work on the same project at the same time with the goal of making one another sound as polished as possible. This is pure collaboration.

When students work together they learn by sharing and copying from one another. Copying, which is how we learn to speak and write, is the most natural method for learning skills. Students have a great ability to inspire one another because they view peer achievements as attainable. This is why attendance at youth music festivals, competitions or eisteddfods is so valuable. Seeing excellence energises, which gives cause for optimism and hope. Self-imposed boundaries regarding potential fall away. This is a phenomenon I often have witnessed in my career as a music teacher. High achievers raise the bar and send messages to others that "you can do this too." I've witnessed school ensembles that reached new heights and set off chain reactions of improvement in other schools.

A wonderful example of peer inspiration is the Australian festival 'Generations in Jazz'. Each May, school jazz ensembles from around the country converge on the regional city of Mount Gambier in South Australia to participate in competition, concerts, and workshops. The presence of Australian jazz legend James Morrison inspires throughout with his phenomenal musical skill and storytelling ability. But in the main it is the students who inspire one another to reach higher and higher. An inspiration principle is at work here—the closer the age of the role model to the student, the greater the possibility for the fire of inspiration to spark. Consequently the past twenty-five years of this festival have witnessed significant growth in the number of student musicians participating - almost 3000 in 2013, and an equally impressive rise in the quality of the music being produced. First-time participants are typically astonished that likeminded peers from schools around Australia can play jazz so well. When home again these children get busy with their teachers and set about to reach the standards witnessed in Mount Gambier. Generations in Jazz presently involves more than two thousand participants and continues to grow.

Meaningful projects taking place over time and involving various forms of group and individual activity are the most promising vehicles for learning. - Howard Gardner (57)

The music world is filled with stories of vital collaboration in which the group outcome is greater than its individual parts. Some people create alone, but often the best creative products result from teamwork.

Creative achievers tend to cluster in societies and subgroups that share their interests, but there is good collaboration and bad collaboration. What was special about Miles Davis's groups, which made so many classic recordings in the late 1950s, including *Kind of Blue,* was that Davis deliberately chose musicians who had different skill sets than his. Prior to a recording session Davis would informally outline his thoughts and ideas to the band, trusting in their ability to interpret and create. This lack of structure and certainty cultivated a heightened listening state and an acute sense of nonverbal communication within the group. Davis worked with arranger and jazz pianist Gil Evans, another prime figure of the 1950s cool school. Evans operated a virtual open house at his New York apartment where likeminded individuals, including Davis, dropped in to share and experiment with musical ideas. Evans's open house was a crucible for creativity.

In the early 1940s, the beboppers gathered at Minton's Playhouse in Harlem to play their brand of music. They were tremendously supportive of one another's creative efforts and established a culture of experimentation. There was friendly competition on the stage but competition in the true sense wherein the likes of Charlie Parker, Dizzy Gillespie, and Bud Powell sought to bring out the best in one another. This group had a culture of playing around with ideas and expressing new thoughts without the inhibiting effects of being afraid of being wrong. They admired individualism and self-expression, and everyone contributed distinctive musical ideas. As Lester Young said to a young Max Roach, "You can't join the throng 'til you write your own song." Great groups become their own worlds. Children thrive when they are surrounded by likeminded peers, just as adults do. Being with others of similar ability is motivating and stimulating and enables children to progress at their optimal rate.

Group collaboration, however, is not always positive and empowering. Mozart never seemed to find his soul group but rather was an object of jealousy and envy among his fellow musicians, even when he was a child. Beethoven yearned for artistic understanding but was very much alone as his deafness increasingly excluded him from the outside world.

> *Art! Who comprehends her? With whom can one consult concerning this goddess? - Beethoven*

School cultures that are conformist and mistake-phobic discourage children from taking risks. The Japanese have a saying "the nail that sticks up gets hammered down." Gangs, and even some clubs, pressure all members to be the same. This type of group comprises sycophants who give praise for their own self-seeking purposes, and cynics who by their nature are anti-creative. Group work can be wonderfully empowering. Find groups that are enthusiastic, support your goals, and challenge you to grow. Enthusiasm for life is contagious, but collaboration for its own sake does not work. You must know when to collaborate and with whom.

> *Great spirits have always found violent opposition from mediocrities.*
> *- Albert Einstein*

CHAPTER SIX

MUSIC AND INTELLIGENCE

IQ Versus Intelligence

French psychologist Alfred Binet was sure that if he could identify children with serious learning difficulties he could address these difficulties through early intervention. Originally developed in 1904 and revised in 1916, Binet's concept of the Intelligence Quotient (IQ) became the premier calculating tool for general intelligence. An advocate of the growth-intelligence mindset, Binet believed people could increase their intelligence through intellectual effort and exercise. Binet, however, feared that his theory could be taken out of context. "A few modern philosophers…assert that an individual's intelligence is a fixed quantity, a quantity which cannot be increased," Binet wrote in 1911. "We must protest and react against this brutal pessimism…. With practice, training, and above all, method, we manage to increase our attention, our memory, our judgment and literally become more intelligent than we were before" (58).

Binet's fears were well founded for at that time the English psychologist Charles Spearman was putting forward a theory which argued that intelligence is general, singular, and fixed (59). Spearman's ideas spread, and his intelligence concept has been widely accepted ever since.

IQ testing is still prevalent today. It measures linguistic and analytical skills, spatial orientation, and logical reasoning. It does not measure abilities necessary for art, music, creativity and innovation, dance and athletic ability, the ability to get along with other people, or self-knowledge. Numerous studies have found only a low correlation between IQ and the achievement of goals. Daniel Goleman claims that IQ accounts for only 4 to 6 percent of life achievement while Harvard University's Howard Gardner figures that IQ predicts approximately 6 to 10 percent of career accomplishment.

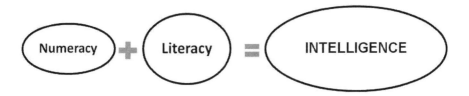

Figure 25: The IQ View of Intelligence

Most school education is IQ centric and places pronounced emphasis on the disciplines of mathematics, science, and literacy. IQ, however, does not represent the full picture of intelligence and does not value the full richness of human intelligence. Ask any student what it means to be smart, and the response almost certainly will be bound to literacy and numeracy. Children value what is tested, and numeracy and literacy are the most frequently tested skills in schools. Literacy, and to a lesser extent numeracy, are essential living skills, but there are other ways of knowing and understanding that also deserve integral places in education.

The IQ model lacks broadness and inclusivity. It is inherently based upon a fixed-intelligence mindset because in IQ theory test scores do not significantly change over time. This flawed theory limits human potential. When we exercise the brain we increase our intellectual potential.

For many years the IQ model of intelligence has been responsible for pushing people away from learning. If you were not successful at numeracy or literacy, you were labelled as stupid. This intellectual scar has led to a high proportion of adults doubting their ability to learn new things and discourages them from engaging in the joys of lifelong learning. Children who adopt a fixed view of intelligence tend to work less hard than others and are more likely to prematurely give up on a task. Statements such as "I'm just not good at this" reveal deterministic and fixed beliefs about learning ability. A lack of belief in one's present ability, or one's potential, results in low self-esteem. Low self-esteem not only is unhealthy for the individual, but also results in all manner of community problems.

> *The greatest evil that can befall man is that he should come to think ill of himself. - Johann Wolfgang von Goethe*

While IQ testing does not include exercises of a musical nature, it appears that musical training in childhood can boost IQ scores, albeit modestly. A 2004 study showed that six-year-old children who received voice or piano lessons had an average increase in IQ of 2.7 points over and above children who received alternative training such as drama, or no extra training (60).

Multiple Intelligence Theory

All cultures deserve a seat at the council of human knowledge.
- Edmund Wade Davis, Canadian anthropologist

Individuals who excel in numeracy and literacy are labelled intelligent, but people refer to musical and other artistic ability as talent; a genetically endowed ability. This dichotomy is evident in the language we use. We *play* music, but we do not *play* mathematics. Can we not be considered intelligent in music? According to Howard Gardner, the answer is yes. In his 1983 book *Frames of Mind: The Theory of Multiple Intelligences,* Gardner broadened the IQ intelligence model into a multidimensional one.

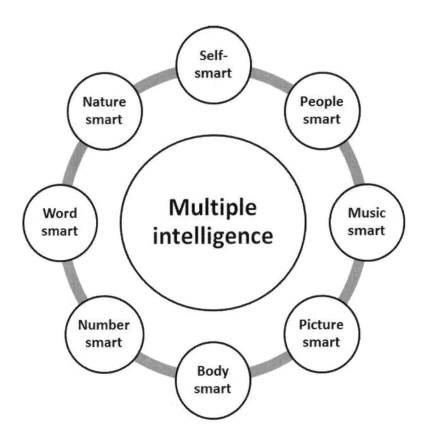

Figure 26: Howard Gardner's Model of Multiple Intelligences

Embracing a multiple intelligence (MI) model is essential for education. Unlike Spearman's unitary concept of intelligence, in the MI model being intelligent in one domain does not necessarily guarantee being intelligent in another. More important, the fact that a child struggles in certain areas does not warrant disregarding his or her intellect.

> *Everybody is a genius. But if you judge a fish by its ability to climb a tree, it will live its whole life believing that it is stupid.*
> *- Albert Einstein*

In the MI model there are many ways to be intelligent (smart). This provides encouragement for students to explore their interests and strengths. [35] The MI model allows all students to discover their passion, to work with intrinsic energy, and to achieve. The question "How smart are you?" becomes "How are you smart?" We are all smart, just in different ways. Nevertheless the average human brain is capable of competently learning and improving in the eight multiple intelligence groups. In addition to this being beneficial to the individual, communities thrive on a human constituency that possesses physical, social, emotional, artistic, and academic skills. As Robert Gagne and Leslie Briggs state in the book *Principles of Instructional Design*, "The basic purpose of education is to bring individuals closer to the goal of optimal use of intelligence and enjoyment of life" (61).

Success cultivates the confidence required to confront weaker learning areas. Warren was a year-eight student in my music class. He had a poor academic record and an even poorer one for behaviour. One day our class had a sing-a-long with me at the piano. Warren sang enthusiastically. "I sing these songs at home with my dad," he said. I invited Warren to sing for me during the break and was impressed with the quality of his voice. I implored Warren to sing for the class, and thankfully he was well received. Next, Warren sang at a school assembly. His peers and teachers reacted more positively toward him, and his behaviour changed noticeably. Warren had found something he did well, something he enjoyed, and something others valued. "Who would have thought...?" more than one teacher commented to me. These teachers implied that because Warren was not an academic –at least according to their definition, it was therefore surprising to see him achieve in music. Through words and actions many teachers reveal a single-intelligence bias.

One of Gardner's multiple intelligences is musical intelligence. How does one measure this? Most people assess their musical intelligence based on their ability to play an instrument or sing. This might be the predominant indicator, but it is not the only one. The ability to compose and respond to music also indicates musical intelligence.

---

35 Clinical psychologist Timothy Sharp, founder of the Happiness Institute in Australia, says that happy people spend more time identifying and utilising their strengths.

Bennett Reimer suggests that Gardner's notion of musical intelligence is not specific enough to describe all of the demands of different musical roles (62). The complex roles in musical intelligence include performer, improviser, composer, listener, teacher, theorist, and musicologist. Perhaps this is why musical ability is so widely distributed in the brain.

Music and the Brain

Neuroscience is the new frontier of twenty-first-century learning, and we are in the midst of an explosion of brain-related research. This has been made possible due to new brain-scanning techniques such as functional magnetic resonance imaging. Much of this research involves music. How does making music, and to a lesser degree listening to music, impact on the brain? Does musical experience change or strengthen parts of the brain? The good news for music education is that neuroscientific studies confirm many of the benefits researchers have determined from observation. It also has presented us with new and deeper understandings in this area of study.

The musician's brain is different from that of the non-musician. Although it does not start out that way substantial changes occur through music training and practice. In particular, music performance activates the motor-control areas of the brain to a high degree.

- The motor cortex, which determines hand movement, is larger for musicians who engage in prolonged instrumental practice (63).
- The cerebellum, which is primarily concerned with motor coordination, is relatively larger in musicians than in non-musicians (64).
- When one performs music, virtually the entire cerebral cortex is active (65).
- The corpus callosum, a bundle of nerve fibres that links the left and right cerebral hemispheres, is significantly larger in musicians than in non-musicians (64).

The last point is interesting. When there is good communication between the two hemispheres, the result is an optimal learning state of integrated thought, a key to higher-level reasoning and creativity. The more both hemispheres are activated, the more neural connections form across the corpus callosum and the faster the data processing. The faster this processing, the more efficiently the intellect can function.

This is clear evidence of the relationship between musical experience and the relative size of brain structures. The greatest brain-plasticity effects occur for musicians who start playing before the age of eight, but the brain continues to change throughout adult life, which results in an increased ability to learn. Increasing proof of brain plasticity challenges key aspects of IQ theory, which views both intelligence and brain structure as being fixed.

The brain is divided into two cerebral hemispheres. The left hemisphere controls the ability to speak, read, and write. However, the right hemisphere is responsible for the musical elements of speech, including intonation, prosody, emphasis, and pitch. Musical processing is even more widely distributed throughout the brain than is speech. Pitch, melody, harmony, and structure tend to be right hemispheric, whereas time structures such as meter, rhythm, and tempo are mainly left hemispheric. The brain processes the emotional response to music mainly in the limbic system and the frontal lobes.

British music educator George Odam states, "Real musical experience should focus on sound rather than symbol so that the sound processors in the right hemisphere can be activated" (66). Reading music, analysis, and intellectualization are all primarily left-hemispheric activities. Unlike formally trained musicians, non-musicians are restricted to emotional response when listening to music and hence activate less of the left hemisphere during listening activity. Music education, then, appears to shift music processing from the right to the left hemisphere (67). Hence, one of the benefits of having a formal musical education is that more of the brain is activated during listening. The cerebral hemispheres are sometimes referred to as 'logic' instead of left and "gestalt" instead of right, because in some people the two are transposed. 'Gestalt' refers to seeing the big picture or perceiving one's environment holistically.

Numerous reports recommend making music as a means of keeping the mind sharp. American neuroscientist Gregory Berns certainly thinks so. Speaking on the BBC's *The Big Idea,* Berns had sixty seconds to present one idea that would change the world for the better. "Everyone should learn to play music," said Berns. He explained:

> It does not matter whether you have talent or if you think you're tone deaf—the simple act of producing a rhythmic or harmonious statement teaches us skills that so often fall by the wayside in modern life. Apart from developing communication skills, making music helps us to listen to each other. It is impossible to make music with other people without listening to your fellow musicians. Making music also develops motor skills. It develops parts of the brain that would otherwise not be used. But most importantly it feels good."[36]

Sing Together and Connect—Oxytocin

One of the most significant neuroscientific contributions in recent times involves the linking of the hormone oxytocin with singing. If there is such a thing as a morality hormone, oxytocin just might be it. Oxytocin is a hormone produced by the brain that contributes to feelings of trust, generosity, and empathy for the people around you. The brain releases oxytocin in large quantities after sexual activity, which bonds couples together. Other stimulants of oxytocin include breastfeeding, massage, dancing together, praying together, and hugging.[37] One of the activities that lead to the highest levels of oxytocin production is singing, and in particular, singing in a choir. When people sing together their brains produce oxytocin, which makes them feel trust, harmony,

---

36 *BBC Magazine,* June 2010; also available as a BBC podcast.
37 Paul Zak (aka, Doctor Love) says humans need eight hugs a day. More oxytocin makes us happier.

and connectedness with the people around them. [38] We have been aware of the health benefits of singing in a choir for some time, such as the 'feel good' factor, the boost in self-esteem, a lowering of stress levels, and socialisation benefits. We know choristers always have felt happier, more energetic, and more relaxed after a rehearsal. Now we understand this from a scientific perspective, as neuroscientific investigation contributes to a growing body of evidence.

Oxytocin is stimulated when people sing together; singing together generates trust and harmony among people. Does oxytocin point to a chemistry of morality? Moral codes are based on empathy, connectedness, and generosity, and these qualities prosper with the release of oxytocin. Will this revelation spark a new impetus for the establishment of school, community, and even corporate choral programs?

Sing psalms and hymns and spiritual songs among yourselves, and make music to the Lord in your hearts. - Ephesians 5:19

Adult Learning

As people grow older they tend to become uncertain about their ability to learn new skills. Certainly we become slower as we age, but older brains still change physically in the same way that younger brains do. When one engages in an activity, new neural connections are formed and myelin develops as a coating on the axon sheath. This only ceases with mental stagnancy; not with age. Bach, Haydn, Beethoven, Brahms, Wagner, Verdi, and Strauss all composed masterworks in their senior adult years. Continued use is the key for the brain to remain healthy and fully functioning. Older people who keep active can continue to challenge younger minds, even in sports. In 2009 Tom Watson almost won the prestigious British Open Championship. The world stopped as the almost sixty-year-old battled it out with men less than half his age. Watson eventually finished second but inspired millions to reset

---

38 According to Paul Zak, 5 percent of the population does not release oxytocin. Reasons include improper nurturing and high stress. Watch out for these people!

the boundaries of possibility for older golfers. Attributing his success to practice, Watson said, "I win golf tournaments by out-preparing other people. I prepare better." Research has shown that when tested on the ability to play a piece of unfamiliar music musicians over the age of sixty who continue deliberate practice for about ten hours a week can match the speed and technical skills of twenty-year-old expert musicians (68). Humans can maintain psychomotor ability for a long time, as long as they continue to practise. In other words, use it or lose it because doing nothing is perilous. [39] Many middle-age people do not learn as many new things as they did in their younger years but rather just maintain existing skills. The brain stays healthy when one engages in new learning, such as learning a new instrument or a new language. Learning something truly new demands intense focus, which keeps the mind sharp.

In terms of improving and maintaining cognitive function music activity is hard to beat. Musical instruction not only retards loss of brain function in the elderly but also supports a range of general health benefits. Professor Nina Kraus from Northwestern University says, "Music training fine tunes the nervous system. Lifelong musical training appears to advantage memory in old age" (69). Anxiety, depression, and loneliness often increase with the aging process, but studies are finding this much less common in people who play music (70). In the mid-sixteenth century, Queen Elizabeth I recognised the therapeutic aspects of playing music. The queen was fond of playing pieces on the spinet from Fitzwilliam's *Virginal Book* and remarked to a visitor, "I play when I am solitary, to shun melancholy" (71). Neurologist Barry Bittman says active participation in making music is the greatest foundation for wellness benefits. In one study, Bittman found that participation in keyboard lessons reduced stress more effectively than watching television or reading (72).

New Horizons for Adults

One exciting program that serves the needs of adult music learners is the New Horizons Music Program. In the late 1980s, Roy Ernst, professor

---

39 A New York study (2001) found that the risk of dementia decreases with a high level of *active* leisure (87).

at Rochester's Eastman School of Music, started to think about developing a music program for retired adults. Traditional community bands mostly catered for people who already could read and play music. In some community ensembles, many of the players had music degrees, and auditions were sometimes required. Roy wanted a beginning-level entry point for adults, just like elementary schools have. In 1991 Roy conducted the first New Horizons band in Rochester, New York, and the program has flourished ever since. Now approximately ten thousand adults are involved in two hundred bands, orchestras, and choirs, in eight countries, under the New Horizons banner.

Three types of beginner usually join New Horizons: those who never have learned an instrument; those who did play but gave up in their school days, so they may not have played for forty-plus years; and those who currently play an instrument—usually a non-band instrument such as piano—but want to learn a new instrument. In June 2012 I accepted an invitation to see the program in person in Rochester and to visit two more hubs in Canada. I was astonished at the purpose, joy, goodwill, and strong relationships that so obviously resulted from this innovative music program. One band I witnessed was an eighty-piece concert band with an average age of seventy-five! It seemed as if age had no hold on these people. In our discussions these elderly musicians told me of their immense satisfaction from making music; they said that playing in the band increased their self-esteem and confidence and gave them a new sense of purpose. The benefit is not just the social aspect, but as Roy says, "Adults have a need for challenging intellectual activity." Music can serve this need better than anything else.

The symbiotic benefits of this program reach far, both economically and socially. A New Horizons program is affiliated with a music school, thereby providing opportunities for young music students to tutor and to learn more about how to teach adults. In return New Horizons members attend tutor concerts and bring family members to join the audience. The host organisation that provides a venue and facilities is well served in return through opportunities that result from their goodwill. Concerts are shared with school groups, conveying a strong message about the lifelong value of making music. Music dealers are serving a vast new market, which as a group is prepared to spend money on quality instruments. [40] In the words of the 1970s British pop band Hot Chocolate, "Everyone's a winner."

Linking Music with Other Learning Areas

> *What's in greatest demand today is not analysis but synthesis—seeing the big picture, crossing boundaries, and being able to combine disparate pieces into an arresting new whole.*
> *- Daniel Pink,*
> *'Drive: The Surprising Truth about What Motivates Us'*

Life is interdisciplinary and multisensory. We learn through all the senses, and we embrace the richness of opportunity and experience that is befitting our multi-intelligent capacity. The richer the brain diet stimulated by the senses the more complex the brain becomes. Learning material presented with pictures and sound provides an emotional attachment that makes information easier to remember and more enjoyable to learn. The most effective memory-building techniques are based on the principle of association, and the strongest associations are emotional. This is multisensory learning.

> *Our senses evolved to work together…which means that we learn best if we stimulate several senses at once.*
> *- John Medina, 'Brain Rules'*

Subject compartmentalisation limits student opportunity to find and observe connection. Schools claim to be holistic by nurturing mental, physical, artistic, and spiritual aspects of the self. In reality, though, the emphasis is very much on mental education, which results in curricula that lack context and are reductionist and fragmented. Interdisciplinary education is a mindset that looks for opportunities to

---

40   In the United States, the over-fifty population is larger than the K–12 population.

make connections among subjects. It encourages thinking about content from different viewpoints and results in a creative synergy and a more personalised education. Students need opportunities to discover connections between disparate bodies of knowledge; this is an axiom of creative thinking. The probability of being creative favours the connected mind. Fostering creativity is an overarching aim in just about every curriculum statement worldwide. Are our general education systems up to the challenge of fostering and sustaining creativity, innovation, and imagination in their students?

> *A real education is the ability to perceive hidden connections between phenomena.*
> *- Václav Havel, Czech playwright and politician*

Many of the world's foremost thinkers were at the intersection of disciplines. Pythagoras of Ancient Greece (570–490 BC) believed that by connecting the natural properties of different doctrines he could discover the secrets of the world. Pythagoras was fascinated by the relationships between music, numbers, the cosmos, and psychology; he was a synthesiser. His great contribution to music was the formation of the diatonic scale, which he developed through mathematical research and scientific investigation. Pythagoras may well be the first person on record who employed music as a therapeutic agent. He believed that beauty and truth combine in music and that music can "quell the passions of the soul" (73). In his philosophy, medicine and therapy were based on music. He called the medicine obtained through music 'purification.' Hence music played an important part in Pythagorean education because music could purify both manners and lives. Those who committed crimes were prescribed "pipe (possibly the panpipe) and harmony" to shape the mind so that it became cultured again. [41] At night Pythagoreans sang certain songs to produce tranquil sleep and induce sweet dreams. In the morning they sang different songs to awaken and prepare for the day. Sometimes the music was instrumental, played on the lyre alone. Pythagoras considered the study of music essential for a rational understanding of God and

---

41   It is unclear whether this referred to a listening or performing activity.

nature. If education is about integrating thought, Pythagoras and the Greek thinkers who followed him led the way.

Possibly the greatest multi-intelligent person (polymath) was the insatiably curious Leonardo da Vinci, who was accomplished at so many things. This list hardly does him justice, but his occupations included painter, musician, inventor, scientist, sculptor, architect, mathematician, and writer. Da Vinci's approach to learning was fully intersectional, cognitive, and sensory. He studied the art of science and the science of art, which generated enormous creativity. He believed that no singular entity should be studied in isolation from context. Like Pythagoras, da Vinci believed that every part of the universe is linked and thus affects every other part. Biologist Charles Darwin regretted not having a greater involvement with music, realising in later life that it would have had a major impact on his intelligence. Today employers such as Microsoft look for creative individuals who can find and make connections between seemingly unrelated bodies of knowledge. Former Australian Prime Minister Paul Keating believes that rationalism without a higher and more conceptual 'poetic strand of life' is incomplete. Keating discusses the power of synthesis between beauty and reason in his 2011 book *After Words*. His inspiration comes from music and beauty. Keating says:

> Music has always been a large part of what makes me tick. When I was listening to music I would always have the pad out to write the ideas down. You listen to a great work, something that was created afresh; you hear the majesty of these works and your head and soul get caught up in them. When that happens you are in for bigger things and you will strike out to be better. [42]

Specialists are not enough. Society needs synthesists and big-picture thinkers. Creativity expert Hideaki Koizumi asserts "Great innovation and new ideas emerge from trans-disciplinary connections" (74).

---

42 Paul Kelly, Oct. 22, 2012. *The Australian.*

Opportunities abound to find connection between music and the other Gardner-defined intelligences.

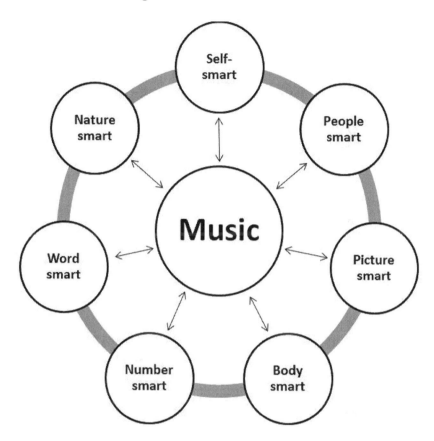

Figure 27: The Connection Between Music and Other Intelligences

Music and Body Smart

Movement as a nonverbal response has always been music's natural partner. The best way to incorporate this is to dance. In addition to the enjoyment factor the wide-ranging benefits of physical exercise on learning are well documented. Dancing is an enjoyable way to move and an enjoyable way to exercise. Engaging in physical activity improves academic achievement, attitude, behaviour, and general health, mood, and sleep quality. Moving creates thinking and generates creative ideas. The cognitive, physical, and well-being effects of exercising to music are greater than when exercising without music (75).

Music can enhance the outcomes of a physical education class. In gymnasiums exercising to music makes a fundamental difference because listening to fast music increases heartbeat. When an appropriate selection of music accompanies an exercise there is a perception that less physical exertion has occurred. In other words, one might run for five miles, but it feels more like four. According to Australian Olympic sports psychologist Peter Terry, when people exercise to music they use one to two percent less oxygen and can run for eighteen percent longer (76). It is not clear why this is so, but it is a useful return on the investment. After exercise, slow music hastens recovery. In addition to offering these physical benefits music helps athletes achieve a state of mind conducive to their tasks. Australian swimmer Kieran Perkins attributed music as a key factor when he won the 1,500-metre Olympic gold medal in Atlanta in 1996. Perkins had a disastrous heat and just managed to qualify for the final. When interviewed about his remarkable turnaround Perkins said that for an hour before the race he focused his mind by listening to music. He won the gold medal in a world-record time. South African Olympian Brendon Dedekind uses pre-race music to energize himself but also for relaxation, focus, and privacy; music fast-tracks Dedekind's emotional state before major sporting events. He says his choice of music is determined by his emotional requirements at the time (77). More recently US swimming superstar Michael Phelps has revealed his preference for listening to hip-hop to prime himself for big events (76).

We are increasingly understanding music's effect on the body. A substantial amount of current medical research involves music and surgery. Post-operative recovery requires lowering heart rate, blood pressure, and body temperature. In clinical trials, music's ability to assist in establishing this desired physiology is encouraging. [43]

We can find opportunities to move in the classroom. I include dance when I teach meter and time signatures. For triple meter I play Johann Strauss waltzes on the piano while students dance around the classroom perimeter, having a ball. On one occasion I was teaching Gregorian chant to a year-nine class. In true monk fashion we proceeded around the school with hands clasped, singing *"Deo Patri sit Gloria!"*

Music and Nature Smart

Look deep into nature, and then you will understand everything better.
- Albert Einstein

The essential lesson of nature is that everything is connected. Immersing oneself in beautiful natural surroundings provides possibilities for creative inspiration. People need beauty as well as bread. Beethoven had a great love of nature and spent hours on solitary walks, drawing inspiration from the fields and trees. Often it was at these times that musical themes came to him. Beethoven himself said, "Nature is a glorious school for the heart."

How happy I am to be able to wander among bushes, under trees, and over rocks; no man can love the country as I love it.
- Beethoven

In a landmark study in 1984, Roger Ulrich found that "post-surgical patients with a window view of trees versus patients with a view of a brick wall had shorter hospital stays, required less medication, and experienced fewer post-surgical complications. Reduced stress, faster recovery, and decreased use of strong painkillers all came from looking at a natural setting as opposed to a blank wall" (78). Simply put, nature heals.

---

43 For further reading see *Music and Medicine Journal*, SAGE Publications.

There is something magical about being outdoors. Fresh air, natural light, a breeze on the skin, natural fragrances, gardens, and landscapes all enhance learning. Children like to learn outdoors. They have a heightened sense of freedom; they let go and explore. What are the opportunities to take a music class outside? I once taught a class with portable keyboards, and, weather permitting, I took them outside. We were a lucky school in that we had open spaces with beautiful large gum trees. School camps provide excellent opportunities to engage in outdoor music-making through campfire songs and outdoor concerts.

Music and Word Smart

Humans sing to express emotional meaning beyond mere words. Because of this emotional connection, when words are combined with music they are easier to learn and easier to remember. *Learning songs* have long been used in primary school classrooms, usually to teach knowledge by rote in mathematics and languages. In 2010 I spoke at a conference in the south of France about music and mathematics and met Colorado-based Susan Gross, an international authority on teaching language acquisition through music. [44] Susan's workshops show musically inexperienced teachers how to integrate songs with knowledge to help students learn faster and remember for longer. The use of song to enhance learning in almost any discipline is limitless. In mathematics there are numerous commercially available songs that teach formulae, mostly involving geometry and counting. Even more rewarding would be to have students write their own songs.

---

44 See http://susangrosstprs.com.

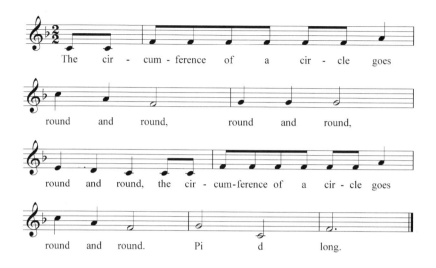

Figure 28: The Circumference Song [45]

We do it effortlessly and learn it in infancy, but using words is still the most complex thing we do. Yet Yehudi Menuhin refers to music as "a form of expression more in touch with our emotional selves and clearer than the abstract nature of words" (79). Nonetheless we need words to make sense of our experiences. Perhaps words cannot describe every experience, but even the attempt deepens the experience.

Events related to emotional experiences are more memorable than non-emotional events. This is why history teachers teach the tragedy of war with fitting music. Who could recollect a movie such as *Schindler's List* separate from its hauntingly poignant theme?

Music and Number Smart

It is often said that music and mathematics are related. Essentially though, music and mathematics are poles apart. Mathematics is about the physical world. It is the first principle of science, and it is used to study the objective, measurable phenomena of our world. In contrast,

45 Alternatively, sing dotted.

music does not and cannot express the physical world. Music is all about human subjective experience, a subject upon which mathematics sheds no light. We use our ears in music and our eyes in mathematics, but both use the mind. Music incorporates sense with reason. Music incorporates structures that reflect mathematical planning, but it is often the deliberate violation of expectation that creates interest.

Music is never reducible to mathematics, but both disciplines are pattern rich so the temptation to draw connection can be irresistible. For some people discovering patterns and connections between music and mathematics is enjoyable. For example, in mathematical index form classical melody phrases conform to the formula $p=2^x$, where p is the phrase length and x is an integer. [46] As discussed in chapter two, the 'sum of seven' rule can assist one to remember key signatures. Chord progressions, intervals, time signatures, metronome markings, sequences, and musical climax points all provide opportunities for finding connection with mathematics.

Music and Picture Smart

Roger Ulrich was involved with another study involving the healing effects of nature. This time the hospital patients did not look at real natural landscapes, only at pictorial representations. Ulrich found these patients had less post-operative anxiety than patients who looked at different types of pictures. A picture is worth a thousand words. Pictures stimulate the mind and refresh our sense of awe and wonder. I have a digital photo frame on my work desk filled with images of beautiful natural landscapes that sequence through in random order. When I seek a cognitive boost a glance at the picture refreshes my mind and inspires me. Pictures connect learning in a powerful way, which is why students learn better from words and pictures than from words alone.

---

46 In other words, phrase lengths are generally two, four, eight, or sixteen measures long.

Only humans create art and can make sense of art. Art contains meaning and is an expression of thought. Art teachers often play music in their classrooms to inspire creativity and help maintain classroom focus. Likewise, some music classes include art. I worked with a teacher who allowed her students to doodle, draw, or colour in when listening to works in the music syllabus. Catherine found that a mixture of visual art and music enhanced reflection, which allowed students to better contemplate the lesson of the day. In a world where the mass media dictate the pace of events to unsuspecting children, Catherine's techniques presented an opportunity to reflect in a creative setting filled with music, art, and no hurried deadlines.

Visual imagery can assist in a conceptual understanding of music analysis. Stephen Malinowski's *Music Animation Machine* provides a scrolling bar-graph score to music. Different colours represent orchestral instruments, durations are depicted by horizontal line length, and pitch by vertical position. This is useful in understanding concepts such as imitation and fugue. My classes really enjoy the numerous works that Malinowski has made available on YouTube, with *Bach's Toccata and Fugue in D Minor* being a particular favourite. [47]

Background Music in the General Classroom and in the Home

Many teachers play background music in the classroom to improve classroom atmosphere and student behaviour. This in turn improves learning outcomes. Carefully selected music can create a classroom dynamic that supports concentration and reflection. Some students study in silence but the majority play music in the background. [48] A major reason they do so is to alter their learning environment. Stressful home environments affect children's ability to learn. [49]

---

47 http://youtu.be/ipzR9bhei_o. 19 million views to date.
48 My research in schools reckons the figure to be about 70 percent.
49 One of the greatest predictors of school performance is emotional stability in the home (88).

In my research, students offer the following reasons for studying with background music.

- "It shuts out distractions, and I get more work done."
- "It helps me feel positive and in a better mood to study."
- "It calms me, and I can stay focused for longer."
- "Time seems to go faster. Maybe I work quicker."
- "It keeps me going for boring homework tasks."
- "It helps with insight, reflection, and creative thoughts."
- "Studying with music is more enjoyable than studying without music."

Selecting Study Music

For music to be successful in a classroom setting some fundamental principles apply. Firstly teachers should not let students select the music. This is not about entertainment but about establishing an environment to improve the conditions for learning. The teacher is trained to understand learning environments, not the students, so this is not a situation in which student choice is a clever idea. The introduction of background music in classrooms requires a period of adjustment, so teachers should expect a settling-in period of about two weeks. Students probably will complain about the choice of music, and generously offer their preferences as a substitute. After a while grumblings will subside, and students will become comfortable with this new addition to the environment. Then the positive effects of music can work their magic in transforming classroom ambience.

While individual and cultural differences, personal history, and environmental circumstances all account for some variation in the way humans respond to music, on the whole music's emotional message is received remarkably consistently. Human emotional response is affected not by musical genre, but by the specific characteristics inherent in the music. In particular, volume, tempo, tonality and texture, and the interaction between these, strongly affect the emotive content of music, hence mood and personal physiological response.

Listening to music can be perceived as calming or stimulating, and all shades in between.

Volume

Volume preference is highly individualistic, but most people have less tolerance for loud music. The louder the music the more attention it demands, so the more distracting it becomes if one is trying to concentrate on a mental task. This is why most people prefer to relax with softer music. Music with sudden dynamic shifts elicits greater emotional responses than music with a narrow volume range. Good study music is emotionally calm. Volume levels between playlist selections also should be consistent. Most playlist compilations include tracks from several sources, so there may be discrepancy in volume levels. Many MP3 programmes such as iTunes have built-in devices designed to condense dynamic variation. Remember to shuffle the playlist to keep it fresh.

Tempo

Fundamentally, faster music stimulates, and slower music calms. Faster music engages us in physical responses, including finger snapping, head nodding, foot-tapping, and dancing. Faster music can be more difficult to study to because, by definition, fast music requires the brain to process more musical events per second. Slow music might cause drowsiness. Music with a tempo slightly faster than the heartbeat works well for study purposes.

Tonality

Tonality refers to the musical scale, or the set of notes on which the music is based. There are numerous scales in world music, but the Western major and minor scales are the most common. These scales are usually identified by a 'happy' or 'sad' tone. For example, 'Twinkle Twinkle Little Star' is in a major key, while a funeral march would be in a minor key. Most children can discern this aspect of music by the age of about six. Generally, major key pieces are more suitable for study music because of their 'happy' tone. However, some minor key pieces should be included in a study playlist because they focus the seriousness of the task at hand. As well as the Western major and minor scales, tonality refers to the modes of Classical Greece. Both Plato and Socrates recognised links between musical modes and character qualities. For example, the Dorian mode was perceived as masculine and courageous, and the Lydian mode as feminine and indolent.

Texture

Texture refers to the thickness of the musical arrangement and whether the music is vocal or instrumental. The simplest texture is monophonic, which is a single melody played either by itself, or with more players in unison. Homophonic music adds vertical support in the form of chords, while polyphonic texture is contrapuntal in nature. The thicker the texture, the more cognitive attention required to process the music. Therefore thickly textured music such as a symphony can be too demanding for studying. More suitable is thin-textured music, perhaps that of a solo acoustic guitar, cello, or piano.

Relationships between musical characteristics create different stimulation thresholds. Harmonised minor music at seventy-two beats per minute (BPM) seems to draw the saddest response from people, whereas non-harmonised major music at 144 BPM draws the happiest response. Music in a major key faster than 144 BPM loses effect, but if it is in a minor key, stimulation continues to increase. Much of music psychology is still a mystery. In *Musicophilia*, Oliver Sacks writes of the paradox when listening to sad music. "It intensifies our experience yet consoles us at the same time," he says. When people are feeling sad, they gravitate toward sad music.

In the home most students study to fast music with lyrics. Lyrics pose a problem. There are some exceptions, such as a Latin text in Renaissance choral music, but the problem with lyrics is that students listen more intently, and even sing along with the lyrics, if only in their mind. This requires cognitive attention and competes with the same brain areas that are trying to comprehend the task at hand. The brain perceives instrumental arrangements of songs without the lyrics in about the same way as it perceives those same songs with lyrics. For studying, instrumental music is a better choice. Background music that incorporates the optimum characteristics for study can be found in many genres, but music from the baroque and early classical period probably satisfies the criteria best. The ability of background music to support study depends on additional factors. First, it depends on the task. Generally, music reduces the boredom of routine work but distracts during complex mental work.

Second, it depends on personality. Introverts require a lower intensity of external stimulation than do extroverts. Studies have shown that introverts perform better than extroverts in a silence condition, whereas the reverse is true in conditions of external stimulation, such as having the radio playing or the television on (80). Introverts are more self-regulatory with their choice of background music than extroverts and will change or even turn off the music depending on the task at hand. Extroverts prefer working in more social and arousing environments. Extroverts report less awareness of self-regulation, preferring rock styles, regardless of task complexity. Extrovert teenage boys are most at risk to choose poor study music.

Third, it depends on one's level of music education. When an understanding of music gets to an academic and 'declarative knowledge' level, the listening experience becomes more left-hemisphere dominant and must compete for attention with the comprehension processors in that part of the brain. Consequently, music specialists such as teachers will cope less well than others when attempting to concentrate on a task while background music is playing. They listen.

Transforming a Concert into a Multidisciplinary Project

Education thrives when learning experiences embrace multiple disciplines and are multi-sensory; when they facilitate mental, physical, artistic, and spiritual growth; and when students design, plan, and exhibit them. One means of achieving this is through projects.

Project-based learning aims to generate as many learning experiences as possible through designing, planning, and exhibiting. The difficulty some teachers might have with this concept is the feeling or expectation that they should be undertaking some of these roles themselves, or at least *should be seen* to be doing so. Students, however, are more highly motivated and more richly rewarded when they do the *doing*. One of the best examples of project-based learning is the concert. Staging a musical concert provides students with a wonderful opportunity to learn and display new skills. A concert provides a public-exhibition point for practical music skills learned in music class or privately. This public display is highly motivating and encourages extra commitment from students. Rather than only being about school grades, this project is authentic and relevant to real life. Through concerts, students find new confidence and self-esteem, and they hone their musical and general skills.

Educational projects such as a music concert should enable students to take responsibility for *all* aspects of the learning and the display. Within the class teachers can organise collaborative committees to take charge of the various elements of concert organisation. The core of music education is learning to sing or play music. Hence, and central to the concert, all students are invited to rehearse an item in preparation for auditions. This involves solo and ensemble work. Class discussion explores the performance opportunities available and suitable for the concert. Students have a choice of repertoire and receive time to work independently and in groups. Original student composition might be favoured in the concert, which addresses the usual balance issue of re-creative music to creative music. The concert might even include other arts such as poetry or dance. The poetry might be thematically connected to the music; the dance might be accompanied by music. An implicit message to students is that the classroom values uniqueness and diversity of student skills and that they should not be afraid to try new ideas. Students become excited because it has become their project. The traditional teacher-led school concert is transformed into a student-led learning project. The teacher remains a source of encouragement and facilitation. If the teacher denies creative and organisational responsibility to the students, valuable learning opportunities will be lost.

Through classroom nomination and, if necessary a ballot, an audition committee is set up. The committee, or the class as a whole, determines the criteria for performance success. The teacher can assist this by performing pieces at different competency levels allowing students to practise applying these criteria. After the audition, the student panel gives feedback to the performance applicants. Another committee takes responsibility for different performance-related matters including:

- Selecting comperes by audition.
- Disseminating concert etiquette expectations.
- Inviting a musician from the local community to perform at the concert, perhaps someone who is unemployed or could benefit from the experience. Concerts can be inclusive.
- Inviting parents and teachers to perform. Students love seeing their teachers on stage, and it helps validate their efforts. I once invited the school groundsman to recite Australian bush poetry in a concert. This strengthened his relationship with the school community.
- Teaching the class a song to be performed with the audience in a grand finale.

A separate team takes responsibility for non-musical aspects of the concert.

- Designing posters, flyers, a newsletter item, and parent invitations.
- Distributing advertising flyers to the local community.
- Delivering a spoken invitation to school staff.
- Choosing stage crew and ushers.

- Arranging box office duties. Selecting a charity to accept the proceeds and inviting a representative to be present at the concert.
- Inviting the home economics department to prepare a supper.
- Inviting the art department to display an exhibit during supper. The art department also might do live sketches of performance artists.
- Inviting the multimedia department to record the concert and edit it for YouTube. Taking photos for the newsletter and school display boards.
- Inviting English classes to write a review of the concert.
- Contacting a school from another country to watch the concert via Skype.
- Finding historical facts about the performance pieces for the compere's notes. (A history subcommittee could do this.)

After the concert, the class analyses the concert's strengths and weaknesses. What feedback did they receive from the audience and how do they gain further feedback about their particular roles? Students reflect in both written and oral expression on their concert roles and the outcomes. What did they enjoy most about the concert experience? What could they do differently next time? The class determines a process to choose a student review for the school newsletter. Finally the concert recording is made available so the experience can be enjoyed again and again. Students bask in the success of their project and are looking forward to the next one. Occasionally the school loudspeakers can play items from the concert and trigger student pride.

The concert project, designed, directed, and owned by the students, has become a cultural feature of the school. Links have strengthened between students and teachers, and with the community and parent body. The project encourages differentiated learning. Students take on different roles, and each role allows rich opportunity for collaboration, initiative, peer critique, research, and practice. Students will come up with more ideas for extending and enhancing their project. There are so many roles available that every student will have the opportunity to be successful in an area of his or her interest.

Music and Emotional Intelligence

In 2009 a report from the UK's authoritative Office for Standards in Education, Children's Services and Skills (Ofsted) criticized music educators for not exploiting music's 'powerful' potential for improving pupils' lives. Ofsted was referring to the emotional-intelligence benefits of music education.

When students engage in project-based learning they get opportunity to develop and practise a range of skills to which traditional schooling does not cater. Relating to peers involves decision-making, expressing opinions, tolerating and accepting different views, regulating emotions, cooperating, and not always getting one's way. These are skills of *emotional intelligence*. Increasingly the world is acknowledging that emotional intelligence—also referred to as EQ, EI, or SEL—is essential for school success, employment success, life success, and daily well-being. [50] EQ comprises the concepts of *self-smart* and *people smart*. In Howard Gardner's model of multiple intelligences these two elements are considered to be distinct intelligences. The influence that making music and listening to music imparts to the development of EQ is considerable.

There was a time when emotions were considered adverse to intelligence. Ancient Greece viewed the ultimate intellectual model as a tripartite psyche with the emotions and the appetite ruled by a superior intellect. People were encouraged to use rational and logical thinking and to suppress emotion when making decisions.

---

50   Emotional quotient (EQ), emotional intelligence (EI), social and emotional learning (SEL).

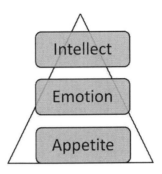

Figure 29: Ancient Greek Model of a Tripartite Psyche

It is impossible, however, to fully separate emotion from intellectual processes. For one thing the brain has more connections going from the (emotional) limbic system to the (intellectual) neocortex than vice versa. This might indicate that emotion influences decision and action more so than rational thought (81). When the rational mind is under stress it is swamped by emotion. Therefore, effective decision-making requires a good degree of EQ. Emotions drive attention, meaning, and memory. Suppression of emotions, which results in repressed emotional build-up, is unhealthy.

> *The little emotions are the captains of our lives, and we obey*
> *them without realizing it. - Vincent Van Gogh*

Music presents an emotional encounter through the medium of sound. Music evokes emotion and emotion affects physiological change. Consequently music has the power to change us not only mentally but also physically. The core of individuality is based on one's unique set of emotions. This is why the world's most popular leisure activity is listening to music, for, in a powerful way music reveals to us our inner self. Hence, music education plays a special role in enhancing emotional intelligence, providing another advocacy opportunity for music educators. In 2009 I met Daniel Goleman at a conference in Washington, DC. Specialising in psychology and brain sciences, Goleman's books on emotional intelligence are internationally renowned. Yet in the course of our discussion Goleman was frank about his own lack of under-standing in regard to music's contribution to EQ. Surprisingly to me the explicit utilisation of music education to advance EQ is yet to be deeply explored.

Music and Self-Smart

Know thyself so that you can be yourself. The final aim is to be.
- D.H. Lawrence [51]

Self-smart people like to learn more about themselves, are generally comfortable with who they are, are secure in their own company, and have a highly perceptive understanding of their feelings and emotions. [52] Humans are social beings, and most of us prefer to spend time in the company of others. Nonetheless, learning to spend time alone is an important skill. Mihaly Csikszentmihalyi says, "Teenagers who cannot bear solitude sometimes have difficulty in later life with tasks requiring serious mental preparation" (31).

Music offers us the chance to sit, relax and listen. Losing ourselves in this way is a form of self-discovery.

> *One of the opportunities art offers us is simply to stand still for a moment and look, or to sit still and listen: the pleasure of being fully present while the ego goes absent and our conscious-ness is filled with something other than ourselves.*
> *- David Malouf, Australian novelist*

James Mursell describes music as "the emotional essence of an experi-ence crystallized in tone" (82). No other art form can elicit emotional reaction to the degree that music can. Stephen Handel explains why music is more emotive than visual art. "Listening is centripetal," he

---

51 Lawrence, D. H. 1922. *Fantasia of the Unconscious.* New York: Thomas Seltzer.
52 Self-smart is also referred to as intrapersonal intelligence.

says. "It pulls you into the world. Looking is centrifugal; it separates you from the world" (83). Music has the ability to enhance our self-knowledge because of our unique emotional response to it. For this reason teachers should encourage children to listen to a wide variety of music. During adolescence children often listen to music that represents rebellion and experimentation. This is normal, but the adolescent heart is also capable of tenderness and gentleness, love and hope, and unbridled joy. When one engages in a range of musical listening experiences one discovers more glorious aspects of the self.

Music appreciation lessons in school often focus on a theoretical framework, with less emphasis on music's emotive content. Teachers can use a descriptor list such as the one below as a prompt in classrooms and private studios to allow students to practise identifying emotion in music.

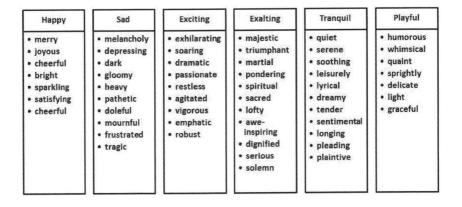

Happy	Sad	Exciting	Exalting	Tranquil	Playful
• merry	• melancholy	• exhilarating	• majestic	• quiet	• humorous
• joyous	• depressing	• soaring	• triumphant	• serene	• whimsical
• cheerful	• dark	• dramatic	• martial	• soothing	• quaint
• bright	• gloomy	• passionate	• pondering	• leisurely	• sprightly
• sparkling	• heavy	• restless	• spiritual	• lyrical	• delicate
• satisfying	• pathetic	• agitated	• sacred	• dreamy	• light
• cheerful	• doleful	• vigorous	• lofty	• tender	• graceful
	• mournful	• emphatic	• awe-inspiring	• sentimental	
	• frustrated	• robust	• dignified	• longing	
	• tragic		• serious	• pleading	
			• solemn	• plaintive	

Figure 30: Emotion Descriptors

Emotion identification and awareness are important aspects of being self-smart. Other self-smart skills include personal reflection, metacognition, stress management, organisation, the ability to resist impulse, and resilience. These are the soft skills of expertise discussed in chapter three.

Know thyself. - Delphic Oracle, Temple of Apollo

The personal security that comes with self-knowledge enables us to be more fully available in relationships with other persons. Consider the model of self-knowledge in the Johari Window in Figure 31. Music helps to reveal more of the self in the great unknown of quadrant four. Other persons reveal to us our blind spots in quadrant two. It may seem ironic, but we need social interactions and relationships to learn more about who we are. We need to be able to relate to others.

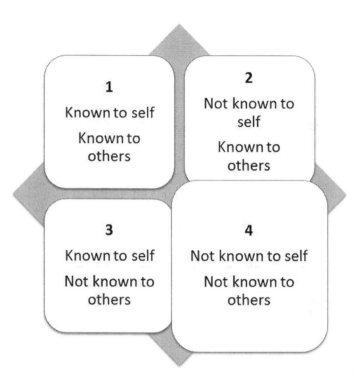

Figure 31: Johari Window (84)

Music and People Smart

What good is math and spelling if the children cannot get along with each other? - Chicago Sun-Times, 2007

In 2007 people in the city of Chicago were becoming increasingly alarmed at the violence and killings among young adults. Why could they not live in harmony? In a series of articles in the *Chicago Sun-Times* the call was made for more emphasis on teaching people skills. Chicagoans were recognising that their schools' narrow intellectual educational focus was not working.

Interpersonal intelligence or being 'people smart' relates to social awareness and relationships. Skills in these areas improve academic learning and have been verified to be more important than IQ in determining professional and life success. [53] Group learning, discussed in more detail in chapter five, is a natural and successful way to develop these skills and deserves a more prominent role in education. Team sport is a useful medium for teaching these skills but inherently creates division through competition. In music ensemble everyone is on the same team. There is a clear sense of purpose and the involvement is not only physical but in comparison with sport more substantially intellectual, emotional, and spiritual (when the musical genre is sacred). If the goal is to maximise the holistic benefits from group activity, music education leads the way.

Participating in ensemble builds relationships that involve trust and respect. Students and teachers must collaborate and negotiate. The group makes decisions regarding artistic goals, and individuals forfeit personal freedoms for the common good. Open communication, social engagement, cooperation, negotiation, and formal and informal tutoring are all part of a well-run ensemble program. Through group musical experiences, students learn to identify the shared emotion of the music, which creates a special empathy among participants.

---

53   Daniel Goleman asserts that as much as 80 percent of adult success comes from EQ.

A FINAL NOTE

When I was eleven years old, I received a 'B' for my Grade Four AMEB classical piano exam. [54] Having achieved better results in earlier grades this came as a disappointment. The real bombshell occurred when my piano teacher informed my mother that she would no longer teach me. My teacher said I had no aptitude for music and that it would be a waste of my mother's money and the teacher's time. A child is so susceptible to adult opinion. If, in my teacher's opinion, I was not musical, then as far as I knew, I was not musical. Fortunately for me, my mother did not accept this verdict. Immediately following the severing of ties with the music teacher my mother phoned the examiner who had given me the grade and requested an honest assessment of my potential. The examiner said the reason for the B was a lack of preparation, but there was plenty about my playing to suggest that I should continue. There was no reason I could not do well, he said, and he even offered to teach me himself. As for the lack of preparation for the exam, he was right. Even at my young age, I had suspected this would be a problem.

During that year, despite my inconsistent practice and inattention to detail, I still received praise from the teacher. When I made errors, she classified them as unimportant little 'slips,' so in a sense she encouraged me to be careless. With my new teacher the practice climate changed considerably, and he termed my slips as mistakes not to be tolerated. He showed faith in my ability so I worked with greater effort. I progressed well and that year, after skipping Grade Five, received an A+ for

---

54   This is the Australian version of the British ABRSM examination system.

Grade Six followed by more excellent results in the higher grades. The circumstances that had led to this positive outcome could well have been the death knell for my life in music. A combination of affirmative action by my mother and the new teacher had me back on track before I could dwell on an apparent lack of musical aptitude.

On another occasion, and at a similar age, I was asked to sing a role in *Oliver* for the school play. I thought I sounded acceptable but judging from the laughter and the ridicule from the all-boys-school audience (including the teachers) my opinion was obviously rose coloured. Humiliation aside, what exasperated me was the lack of feedback from those who had chosen me for this role. Was I out of tune, or was it my tone, lack of volume, or diction? I needed to know the problem. Consequently my stage debut was short-lived. I was discarded for another boy and thrown to the 'lions'. My self-image, largely based on being good at music, shattered that day, and I would not sing again for more than ten years. One day I realised I had to overcome this fear. If I were to become a better music teacher, I had better get over it.

The point of these stories is that teachers and parents should be cautious when evaluating children and clear when providing feedback. With sustained application over a period of time, who knows what a child can achieve. Potential is difficult to assess for those who start out the cleverest do not always end up the cleverest. Grades only can provide a snapshot of current skill level. Work makes the difference and unlike genetic factors is in the control of the person.

> *I have always maintained that excepting fools, men did not differ much in intellect, only in zeal and hard work.*
> *- Charles Darwin* [55]

Darwin's mindset encapsulates the essential message of this book. With a growth-mindset, and repeated and sustained effort, we can substantially improve in our endeavours. If musical achievement is the

---

55 Darwin wrote this in a letter to his cousin Francis Galton.

endeavour, the best predictor of success is the quality and quantity of practice time.

The lessons in learning music are lessons for learning in life. There is little that reaches the level of complexity that making music demands and possibly no other activity that asks so much of our multi-intelligent capacity. Today, other disciplines study musicians in the hope of improving performance in their respective domains.

> *Musicians are in an excellent position to teach us about better ways to become and remain expert performers in health care, and ways for our teachers and mentors to help us do that.*
> *- Frank Davidoff (85)*

Music-making is unique and vital to the human condition. Music is humane and social; it is the tonal bridge-building fabric of society. School communities are ideally placed to promote a sense of community through music. The business world has begun to recognise the value of generating group cohesion through the arts. In 2010 I presented in the African country of Malawi. As I wandered through the grounds of my hotel I noticed a group of staff near the rear of the property, singing together. They told me the management was holding a competition for the best song that incorporated the company mission, so they had formed a choir to participate. "This is voluntary, but all the workers are involved," one of them said. The 2012 BBC community choir series *Sing While You Work* demonstrates that singing in the workplace improves employee confidence, communication skills, and teamwork.

> *Music promotes group cohesion. Music is present in all kinds of gatherings—in dancing, religious rituals, ceremonies—thereby strengthening interpersonal bonds and identification with one's group. Music favours emotional communion.*
> *- Isabelle Peretz, psychology professor*
> *at the University of Montreal (86)*

Music plays a dynamic role in energizing the self. Music gives us a reason to live; a reason to be, providing us with a constant source of experience. Music is, as Beethoven said, a revelation "greater than all wisdom and philosophy." I invite you to join with me to spread this message. Learn, teach, and make music!

References

1. Colvin, G. 2008. *Talent is Overrated: What Really Separates World-class Performers from Everybody Else.* London: Nicholas Brealey.
2. Howe, M. J. 1999. *Genius Explained.* Cambridge: Cambridge University Press.
3. Gladwell, M. 2008. *Outliers.* London: Penguin.
4. Sloboda, J. et al. 1996. "The Role of Practice in the Development of Performing Musicians." *British Journal of Psychology* 87:399–412.
5. McPherson, G. E. and Renwick, J. M. 2001. "A Longitudinal Study of Self-Regulation in Children's Musical Practice." *Music Education Research* 3:169–86.
6. O'Neill, S A. The Role of Practice in Children's Early Musical Performance Achievement. In H Jørgensen and A C Lehmann [ed.] *Does Practice Make Perfect? Current Theory and Research on Instrumental Practice.* 1997, pp. 53-70.
7. McPherson, G. E. and McCormick, J. 1999. "Motivational and Self-Regulated Learning Components of Musical Practice." *Bulletin of the Council for Research in Music Education* 141:98–102.
8. Sternberg, R, J & Grigorenko, E. L. *Teaching for Successful Intelligence to Increase Student learning and Achievement.* Arlington Heights: Skylight.
9. Brown, E., Campbell, K., and Fischer, L. 1986. "American Adolescents and Music Videos: Why Do They Watch?" *Gazette* 37:19–32.

10. Levitin, D. 2006. *This Is Your Brain on Music: The Science of a Human Obsession.* New York: Penguin.
11. Berger, R. 2003. *An Ethic of Excellence: Building a Culture of Craftsmanship.* Portsmouth: Heinemann.
12. Coyle, D. 2009. *The Talent Code.* New York: Bantam Books.
13. Jorgensen, H. 1997. Time for Practising? Higher Level Music Students' Use of Time for Instrumental Practising. In H Jørgensen and A C Lehmann [ed.] *Does Practice Make Perfect? Current Theory and Research on Instrumental Practice.* 1997, pp. 123-140.
14. Porter, L. 1998. *John Coltrane: His Life and Music.* In Mathieson, K. 1999. *Giant Steps: Bebop and the Creators of Modern Jazz.* Edinburgh: Payback.
15. Weisberg, R. W. 2006. *Creativity: Understanding Innovation in Problem Solving, Science, Invention, and the Arts.* Hoboken: John Wiley & Sons.
16. Ericsson, K. A., Krampe, R. T., and Tesch-Romer, C. 1993. "The Role of Deliberate Practice in the Acquisition of Expert Performance." *Psychological Review* 100:363–406.
17. Zimmerman, B. and Kitsantas, A. 2002. "Comparing Self-Regulatory Processes Among Novice, Non-Expert, and Expert Volleyball Players: A Microanalytic Study." *Journal of Applied Sport Psychology* 14:91–105.
18. Suzuki, S. 1998. *His Speeches and Essays.* Miami: Warner Bros.
19. McPherson, G. E. 2001. "Commitment and Practice: Key Ingredients for Achievement During the Early Stages of Learning a Musical Instrument." *Council for Research in Music Education* 147:122–127.
20. James, W. 1899. Talks to *Teachers on Psychology; and to Students on Some of Life's Ideals.* New York: Henry Holt and Company.
21. Smith, H. W. 1961. *From Fish to Philosopher.* Garden City: Doubleday & Company, Inc.
22. Ullen, F. et al. 2005. "Extensive Piano Practising Has Regionally Specific Effects on White Matter Development." *Nature Neuroscience* 8:1148–50.
23. Duke, R. A. et al. 2009. "Effects of Early and Late Rest Breaks During Training on Overnight Memory Consolidation of a

Keyboard Melody." *The Neurosciences and Music III: Disorders and Plasticity: Ann. N.Y. Acad. Sci.* 1169: 169–172.

24. Nishida, M. and Walker, M. P. 2007. "Daytime Naps, Motor Memory Consolidation and Regionally Specific Sleep Spindles." *PLOS ONE* 2(4).

25. Simmons and Duke, R. 2006. "Effects of sleep on performance of a keyboard melody." *Journal of Research in Music Education,* 54, 257–269.

26. BBC News. 2011. Sleeping Longer Helps Athletes Reach Peak Performance.   http://www.bbc.co.uk/news/health-13974130 (accessed July 2, 2011).

27. Doidge, N. 2007. The Brain that Changes Itself: Stories of Personal Triumph from the Frontiers of Brain Science. New York: Viking.

28. McPherson, G. E. 2005. "From Child to Musician: Skill Development During the Beginning Stages of Learning an Instrument." *Psychology of Music* 33:5–35.

29. Gallwey, T. W. 1974. *The Inner Game of Tennis.* New York: Random House.

30. Robinson, K. 2009. *The Element.* New York: Viking.

31. Csksentmihalyi, M. 1990. *Flow: The Psychology of Optimal Experience.* New York: Harper Perennial.

32. BBC Newsround. 2007. Kids Live with No TV for 14 days! http://news.bbc.co.uk/cbbcnews/hi/newsid_6750000/newsid_6758300/6758315.stm (accessed June 19, 2007).

33. Keller, C. March 24, 2010. Too Busy on Facebook to Do Homework.   http://www.adelaidenow.com.au/news/south-australia/too-busy-on-facebook-to-do-homework/story-e6frea83-1225844477121 (accessed March 25, 2010).

34. Jan, T. April 24, 2011. Tangled in an Endless Web of Distractions. http://www.boston.com/news/education/higher/articles/2011/04/24/colleges_worry_about_always_plugged_in_students (accessed April 25, 2011).

35. Gorlick, A. August 24, 2009. Media Multitaskers Pay Mental Price, Stanford Study Shows. http://news.stanford.edu/news/2009/august24/multitask-research-study-082409.html (accessed August 26, 2009).

36. Email Has Made Slaves of Us. *Australian Daily Telegraph,* June 16, 2008. [As reported by Ariely, D. *Predictably Irrational.* Harper. 2008. p255.]

37. Gentile, D. A. and Walsh, D.A. 2002. "A Normative Study of Family Media Habits." *Journal of Applied Developmental Psychology* 23:157–178.

38. Pink, D. 2009. *Drive: The Surprising Truth About What Motivates Us.* New York: Riverhead Books.

39. Kohn, A. 1993. *Punished by Rewards.* Boston: Houghton Mifflin.

40. Amabile, T. 1998. "How to Kill Creativity." *HBR.* Sept./Oct.:74–78.

41. Hallam, S. 2001. "The Development of Metacognition in Musicians: Implications for Education." *BJME* 18:27–39.

42. Collins, S. J. June 22, 2011. Uni Students Struggle with Degree Ennui. http://www.theage.com.au/national/uni-students-struggle-with-degree-ennui-20110621-1gdk7.html (accessed June 23, 2011).

43. Benware, C. and Deci, E. 1984. "Quality of Learning With an Active Versus Passive Motivational Set." *American Educational Research Journal* 21:755–765.

44. Elliott, D. 1995. *Music Matters: A New Philosophy of Music Education.* New York: Oxford University Press.

45. Duckworth, A. L. and Seligman, M. E. 2005. "Self-Discipline Outdoes IQ in Predicting Academic Performance of Adolescents." *Psychological Science* 16:939–944.

46. Goleman, Daniel. 1997. *Emotional Intelligence: Why It Can Matter More Than IQ.* New York: Bantam Books.

47. James, W. 1890. *Principles of Psychology.* New York: Holt.

48. Covey, S. 1994. *First Things First.* New York: Simon & Schuster.

49. Glenn, K. A. (1999). Rote vs. note: The relationship of working memory capacity to performance and continuation in beginning string classes. (PhD diss., the University of Northern Colorado). Dissertation Abstracts International, 60/04, 1010. (University Microfilms No. 9927738) in McPherson, G. E. and Parncutt, R. (Eds) *The Science and Psychology of Music Performance: Creative Strategies for Teaching and Learning.* (New York: Oxford University Press. 2002), 102.

50. G. E. and Parncutt, R. (Eds). 2002 *The Science and Psychology of Music Performance: Creative Strategies for Teaching and Learning.* New York: Oxford University Press.

51. Williamon, A. 1999. "The Value of Performing from Memory." *Psychology of Music* 27:84–95.

52. McPherson, G. E. 1993. "Factors and Abilities Influencing the Development of Visual, Aural and Creative Performance Skills in Music and their Educational Implications." PhD thesis, University of Sydney, Australia. *Dissertation Abstracts International* 54:1277A.

53. De Bono, E. 1995. *Serious Creativity.* New York: HarperCollins.

54. Limb C. J. and Braun A. R. 2008. "Neural Substrates of Spontaneous Musical Performance: An FMRI Study of Jazz Improvisation." *PLOS ONE* 3(2):e1679. doi:10.1371/journal. pone.0001679.

55. Dobinson, C. 1969. *Jean-Jacques Rousseau.* London: Methuen.

56. Green, L. 2002. *How Popular Musicians Learn.* Burlington: Ashgate.

57. Gardner, H. 1991. *The Unschooled Mind.* New York: Basic Books.

58. Binet, A. 1911. *Modern Ideas About Children.* [Published in English 1984 Menlo Park: Suzanne Heisler.]

59. Spearman, C. 1904. "General Intelligence: Objectively Determined and Measured." *American Journal of Psychology* 15: 201–293.

60. Schellenberg, E. G. 2004. "Music Lessons Enhance IQ." *Psychological Science*, 15:511–514.

61. Gagne, R. M. and Briggs, L. J. 1979. *Principles of Instructional Design.* New York: Holt, Rinehart and Winston.

62. Reimer, B. 2004. "New Brain Research on Emotion and Feeling: Dramatic Implications for Music Education." *Arts Education Policy Review* 106:4.

63. Amunts, K. et al. 1997. "Motor Cortex and Hand Motor Skills: Structural Compliance in the Human Brain." *Human Brain Mapping* 5:206–215.

64. Schlaug, G. et al. 1998. "Macrostructural Adaption of the Cerebellum in Musicians." *Society Neuroscience,* Abstracts 24:2118.

65. Weinberger, N. M. 1998. "The Music in Our Minds." *Educational Leadership.* 56:3:36-40.
66. Odam, G. 1995. *The Sounding Symbol.* Cheltenham: Stanley Thornes.
67. Ono, K. et al. 2011. "The Effect of Musical Experience on Hemispheric Lateralization in Musical Feature Processing." *Neuroscience Letters* 496:141–145.
68. Ericsson, K. A. et al. July, 2007. The Making of an Expert. http://hbr.org/2007/07/the-making-of-an-expert/ar/1   (accessed August 10, 2007).
69. Pedersen, T. Musicians Less Prone to Some Age-Related Memory, Hearing Problems. http://psychcentral.com/news/2011/05/13/musicians-less-prone-to-some-age-related-memory-hearing-problems/26151.html (accessed May 14, 2011).
70. Lee, Y. Y., Chan M. F., and Mok E. 12010. "Effectiveness of Music Intervention on the Quality of Life of Older People." *Journal of Advanced Nursing* 66:2677–2687.
71. Bie, O. et al. 1899. *A History of the Pianoforte and Pianoforte Players.* London: J.M. Dent & Co.
72. DeNoon, D.J. Feb 8, 2005. Making Music Soothes Stress. http://www.cbsnews.com/2100-500368_162-672401.html (Accessed Feb 10, 2005).
73. Bernard, R.W. 1958. *Pythagoras: The Immortal Soul.* New York: Columbia University.
74. Koizumi, H. 2001. "Transdisciplinarity." *Neuroendocrinology Letters* 22:219–221.
75. Ohio State University. March 24, 2001. A Little Music With Exercise Boosts Brain Power, Study Suggests. http://research-news.osu.edu/archive/hartsong.htm (accessed October 12, 2011).
76. Jeffrey, N. July 13, 2012. Music the Fuel for Performance Overdrive by Olympic Athletes. http://www.theaustralian.com.au/arts/music/music-the-fuel-for-performance-overdrive-by-olympic-athletes/story-fn9d2mxu-1226424849410 (accessed July 14, 2012).
77. Dedekind, B. 2010. Motivation and the Place for Music in Swimming. http://swimming.about.com/od/sportpsychology/

qt/Music_Swimming_Motivation.htm (accessed December 29, 2010).

78. Ulrich, R. S. 1984. "View Through a Window May Influence Recovery from Surgery." *Science* 224:420–421.

79. Menuhin, Y. 1979. *The Music of Man.* New York: Simon & Schuster.

80. Furnham, A. and K. Allass, K. "The Influence of Musical Distraction of Varying Complexity on the Cognitive Performance of Extroverts and Introverts." 1999. *European Journal of Personality* 13:27–38.

81. Michels, P. 2001. *The Role of the Musical Intelligence in Whole Brain Education.* D.Mus Thesis, unpublished, University of Pretoria.

82. Mursell, J. 1934. *Human Values in Music Education.* Vancouver: Silver, Burdett & Co.

83. Handel, S. 1989. *Listening: An Introduction to the Perception of Auditory Events.* Cambridge: Bradford Books.

84. Luft, J. P. A. 1970. *Group Processes: An Introduction to Group Dynamics.* Palo Alto: National Press Books.

85. Davidoff, F. 2011. "Music Lessons: What Musicians Can Teach Doctors (and Other Health Professionals)." *Annals of Internal Medicine* 154:426–429.

86. Peretz, I. 2002. "Brain Specialization for Music." *The Neuroscientist* 8:372–380.

87. Scarmeas, N. et al. 2001. "Influence of Leisure Activity on the Incidence of Alzheimer's Disease." *Neurology.* Vol. 57:2236-2242.

88. Medina, John. 2008. *Brain Rules.* Seattle: Pear Press.

Made in the USA
San Bernardino, CA
29 May 2014